AF443479

A GUIDE TO
SELF-DISRUPTION

www.amplifypublishinggroup.com

A Guide to Self-Disruption: Five Principles and a Daily Process to Transform Your Life

Images used under license from Shutterstock.com.

For more information, please contact:
Amplify Publishing, an imprint of Amplify Publishing Group
620 Herndon Parkway, Suite 220
Herndon, VA 20170
info@amplifypublishing.com

Library of Congress Control Number: 2023920347

CPSIA Code: PRV0124A

ISBN-13: 978-1-63755-865-2

Printed in the United States

*This book is dedicated to all imperfect humans—those
of us who, despite our many flaws, desperately desire to
make the most out of a life lived in service to our family,
friends, coworkers, communities, country, and God.*

A GUIDE TO SELF-DISRUPTION

FIVE PRINCIPLES AND A DAILY PROCESS TO TRANSFORM YOUR LIFE

KLINT GUERRY

TABLE *of* CONTENTS

FOREWORD

I have spent my life researching weirdos.

After spending 12 years at Harvard researching the impact of a positive brain on performance, I traveled to more than 50 countries attempting to understand why some people are so different. Why do some people respond to the world differently than the average person? Why can some people change while others keep making the same mistakes? Why is it that some people are not debilitated by trauma but actually get stronger as a result? Why are some people's success rates rising while others around them in the same environment are stagnating? Why are some people able to remain optimistic and resilient when others break? I study the positive outliers—the weirdos—who teach us important things about the possibility for change. **I study weirdos like Klint Guerry.**

In my work I research how small shifts in mindset or habit create massive and quantifiable long-term impacts on people. It is stunning how even small changes can completely transform the trajectory of someone's life. I had already been studying the role of journaling upon long-term levels of success and happiness when I became friends with Klint. Previous research has shown that the practice of consistent journaling not only decreases stress, improves our emotional immune system, and raises happiness, but importantly we have found that journaling helps the brain remap meaning. There are meaningful inter-actions and ideas that occur to us every day, but if the brain is using its finite resources to process just the mundane or the negative or the threats coming in, we completely miss all that meaning. When people start journaling, they scan for meaning and then record the meaning, which increases the likelihood of retention. But, crucially, the brain can't tell much difference between visualization and actual experience, so **by journaling you effectively double the most meaningful parts of your day.** Over a period of even just 21 days, your brain connects the dots between those nodes of meaning, and suddenly you have a clear trajectory of meaning running throughout your life—which changes everything. What Klint taught me is that by using Gueri Notes, you can magnify that impact by returning to the journal to analyze patterns. By understanding yourself better, you increase your ability to change consciously and effectively.

They say that research is really me-search—we are interested in studying our own potential for growth and what gets in our way. We study what we care about. The Gueri Notes Process and *A Guide to Self-Disruption* are tools that allow you to turn research into me-search. Each helps you to identify efficiently how you can move forward, track progress, and stop what is getting in your way. Disruption leads to change, which can lead to a revolution. The Gueri Tools are one of the best ways I've seen for going deep to create long-lasting change to what happens next in your life.

Shawn Achor

New York Times bestselling author
of *Big Potential* and *The Happiness Advantage*

PREFACE

"I loved the content, but it would have made a better article. It certainly didn't need 250 pages dedicated to the topic." JOE STALLARD

These words have echoed in my mind regularly over the decade I have invested in writing *A Guide to Self-Disruption*. Joe and I have worked together for more than 20 years, and he is a learner like me. We have shared more books and learning experiences than I can count. One such time, when I inquired about a book he had just finished reading, his response was, "I loved the content, but it would have made a better article . . ."

When I made the decision to embark on a writing journey of my own, it was important to keep it simple. A long article, so to speak, and one that won't overwhelm someone who is not an avid reader. Furthermore, a short book is perfectly appropriate as, outside of being a workday-wearer of a bow tie, I am

a pretty plain vanilla, normal person. I am a husband to Natalie,
a father to three, a friend, an employee, a leader, a peer, a son,
a brother, a church member, a person who tries hard, one who
has flaws and one who struggles. In other words, I am a human.

On May 31, 2004, I made a decision that changed the trajectory of my life. This book is written to share that spark with you—the process itself and the subsequent lessons. It is not my intention to impose the exact behaviors as a "best practice" but rather to share my story, the learning, and inspire you to either literally or metaphorically write your own. At its best, this book will live alongside you as a guide as you walk the path of life. This is how I use it, and I have found it to be a valuable companion.

I was one month shy of my 26th birthday, and I had absolutely no idea on that random Monday morning in Dallas, Texas, that the process and behaviors I was committing to that day would have such a profound impact on my future, both personally and professionally. In fact, through the lens of hindsight, it seems nothing short of a miracle. My life was a mess (always had been), and whether it was simply dumb luck or something much, much deeper that sparked this journey, it was on this day that I learned to shift from a state of perpetual self-destruction to a life dedicated to positive, productive growth through self-disruption.

This book serves as the jump start, accountability partner or spark of inspiration to do the things that most of us already know that we should do. Truly, the only thing magical about it is that it forces us to dig deep, to be completely honest with ourselves, to reevaluate and to focus or refocus how we spend and share our time, energy and resources. We are committing to the arduous work of radical self-disruption for the purpose of shaping ourselves into people who achieve the extraordinary in life.

The Promise

I get asked a lot about the names on my products and logo, Gueri Notes and Gueri Fine Tools for Development. You can clearly see on the cover that my last name is spelled "Guerry." The original French spelling of my last name is "Gueri." I do not speak French, but I was thrilled to discover that this word means "cured, healed, or restored." This book and the Gueri Notes Process itself have done and continue to do precisely these things in my life. God willing, my hope is to continue to add to the books and products offered by Gueri Fine Tools, for me and others like me, in need of healing, restoration, inspiration, growth and development. Thus, there seemed to be no better name.

The Name

I would be remiss if I didn't take a moment to explain the first chapter, The Letter. Over the many years of working on this project—an hour or two at a time while lying in bed, on an airplane, or in a coffee shop, or while sitting at that terribly uncomfortable desk in a hotel room—there has always been a group of men and women behind the scenes advising me along the way. I have made every effort to thank each of them in the acknowledgments section. They have been instrumental to the fact that I haven't given up and have remained committed to seeing this through despite seasons of frustration. Their advice and counsel is reflected in this work. While I selected one member of my team of mentors to be the physical example of a specific principle, they each have lived lives that embody all five. In many ways, *A Guide to Self-Disruption* is an amalgamation of their personalities.

Although each supplied unique ideas, there was one thing that all insisted on from the beginning—that I include some portion of my story. I must admit this was not an easy thing for me to do, but not because I am worried or prideful about you knowing. I really want this journey to be about you and not about me. However, all felt it necessary for me to share a snippet of the backstory in order for you to gain a better understanding of the origin of the Gueri Notes Process and this book. I wrote and rewrote the story countless times but could never quite settle on something that felt right. One day it struck me that the best way to tell the story and to honor my dear friend who inspired this work was to write him a letter of gratitude.

BEST WISHES ON YOUR JOURNEY.

The Letter

My Dear Friend,

Reach back in the recesses of your mind to October of 2012. Waiting for a flight home to Dallas in the DC airport, I had my travel-worn notebook and you had the morning paper. "How many of those notebooks do you have?" you asked over the downturned corner of *The New York Times*. To which I replied that I really had no idea, but "it's a big number." At the time, I had been following this disciplined daily regimen with my notebook for eight years, so "a big number" was an accurate representation. That question launched an hours-long conversation about how I use the notebooks as tools for managing life, capturing precious moments, and pursuing personal and professional growth.

As we taxied to our gate in Dallas, you challenged me to do two things: 1) explain the notebook process that I use every day in such a way that it can be shared with others, and 2) reflect on the years of notebooks that I had at the time—the lessons learned, the wisdom—and refine the whole into a few, clear principles. A dozen years later, I am writing to say thank you.

I knew the task would be hard, but I didn't expect it to be so revealing. Francis Bacon was right in that reading makes a full man, talking makes a ready man, but writing makes an exact man. Your challenge both refined me and clarified my understanding of the notebooks. I now know that these notebooks, the steps and the principles have been at the heart of achieving the life I enjoy today. You see, there is a lot that you don't know about me, Friend. Not because I am embarrassed, but rather because I have never felt it relevant to share. But your challenge also helped me realize that I need to share my story for two very important reasons. First, the story provides context for the genesis of, and the transformative nature of, this process. Without the story, it is difficult to grasp the magic. And, second, I have learned thousands of lessons over the years, but one ranks somewhere near the top: all of us have a story. They are all important, and there is always someone who can relate to, learn from, and be inspired by your experiences. It is those experiences, both positive and negative, that make us who we are, and the wisdom gained from our scars shouldn't be covered over. It should be shared. So, here goes the leap into the frightening pool of vulnerability.

My mother and father were both tragic alcoholics. Best I can tell, Dad was already a slave to his addiction by the age of 18, but, thankfully, he was high functioning. He found early success as a dashing and intelligent banker in West Texas. By 30, he was the president of a bank in a small Texas town, which at the time was a position second only to the mayor in power and prestige. Mom was the perfect housewife.

She tended to the needs of my brother and me, kept the house immaculate, and met my father at the door in the evening with a 7 and 7. I was too little to know the rest of the story, but by the age of four we began moving around a lot. It was then I noticed strange things started happening with Mom and Dad. Over time, I learned that the bank was closed by the Fed in the early 1980s. He moved us from town to town trying to find a way to put the pieces back together, but it was already too late. It was the beginning of the end.

When I was eight, my brother went off to college, my parents hit the bottle to soothe their pain, and I fended for myself. Overnight, it was just the three of us. It was during this time that I learned how to sell, a skill that has served me well. Few things are more difficult than attempting to reason with two drunken people intent on destroying themselves and each other. This was my lot in life in no particular order: keep Mom and Dad alive, try to convince them to see the error in their ways, be in the fight but not physically affected by it, remember to brush my teeth, study for that spelling test, and play a little Wiffle ball with friends in between. Pretty sad to think about now that I have my own children.

Unfortunately, I was unable to help them see the light, and things only deteriorated over time. Mom died from liver failure at 5:50 a.m. on November 28, 1994, when I was 16.

She was just 43 years old. Then, it was just the two of us.

The next two years were my version of hell on earth. Dad threatened suicide, which added a whole new level of complexity and stress to the situation. He didn't work, so we rarely had food, water, or electricity. I remember filling up empty two-liter soda bottles with water from our neighbor's garden hose to use to brush my teeth and wash my face before bed. The meager Social Security checks that came following Mom's death went to Dad's booze and cigarettes. My grandparents, destroyed over the loss of their daughter, tried to get me to move to the country with them, but I refused for fear of what would happen to him. They set up a little checking account for me and deposited $100 a month so that I could eat. But like the Social Security checks, the money was spent at the liquor store. Needless to say, my grades suffered being a parent for my father.

However, a sweet family down the street knew of my situation and gave me a safe place to go when I needed an escape from my reality, a shower to use, and free access to the pantry. Their help outside the school was matched by Debbie Pigg's help inside the school. To say that she was just my high school guidance counselor would be an understatement of epic proportions. I spent many an hour in her office just talking. She looked out for me and did more than I'm sure was allowed. The most important thing, though, was to get me out of my school where I was dangerously close to flunking out, which would have spelled certain doom, and get me enrolled in an alternative high school for troubled youth. I flourished. I graduated. I came to understand that he was not my burden. I got out. Finally, it was just the one of us.

Moving to Dallas a few days before my eighteenth birthday marked the beginning of my long road to recovery as a child of alcoholic parents. My brother gave me a couch to sleep on and got me a job doing manual labor at his friend's company. Despite the fresh start, the next few years were a mess as I clumsily navigated life as an adult with battle-tested survival skills but absolutely no healthy life skills. In an ironic twist, life without chaos required different competencies. Children who grow up in the home of addicts take on many of the same characteristics and habits as their parents, even if they are not addicts themselves. This was certainly true in my case. I didn't know how to live in a world without the constant threat of tragedy or the looming cloud of despair. As a result, I lived well beyond my means, choosing momentary pleasures over stability. Sadly, in my mind, stability was a fantasy.

I was a terrible employee and I changed jobs like socks. Some by choice and others not. I was often late to work, was horribly unreliable, and blamed others rather than maturely accepting responsibility for my failures. I struggled in relationships, didn't pay my bills, and spiraled into my own created chaos. Through the lens of hindsight, I was a tormented young man who found a stable life uncomfortably boring. I unconsciously torpedoed the good for the comforts of the turmoil. It felt like home. And, tragically, it is this same vicious pattern that often results in the children of addicts becoming addicts themselves. BUT—and shout it from the rooftops so that all the world can hear just how happy I am that there's a "BUT" in my story—a perspective of meaningful work, and a stunning beauty named Natalie, functioned as a glorious hammer to shatter the cycle.

My Friend, the passion for my profession is no secret to you, but it wasn't until I dissected "how" I arrived here that I began to understand the depth of my maturation, productivity, and earned success as a result. This incredible family-owned business saw something in me that I didn't know was there. They had higher expectations for me than I had for myself and demanded the discipline, structure, hard work, and dedication that I lacked. They supported my education and encouraged me to finish my undergraduate degree.

As strange as it may seem, this company filled a large part of the void that was left by my parents. They made me want to expect more out of myself and taught me that there is no such thing as the easy way.

Then there was Natalie. I will always remember the first time I saw her. She had just graduated from college and had been with the company only a few days. I thought she was absolutely spectacular. We immediately hit it off, but, much to my chagrin, I was to be placed firmly in the friend zone. It wasn't until a year or so later of growing closer that I wore her down enough to give dating a try. I was convinced from the start that she was the one. I desperately wanted to marry her, but she was just so far out of my league that I had doubts as to whether or not I was the one. Her upbringing couldn't possibly have been more different—a safe and loving family, a strong foundation of faith, a great education, and a firm understanding of the importance of financial responsibility. As a result, she rightfully had high expectations for herself and for others. I loved her so much that I would never expose her to the chaos and uncertainty that I had frustratingly grown so accustomed to.

Threat of loss is a powerful motivator. Faced with these two incredible opportunities—a career that I was passionate about and the woman of my dreams—I committed myself to the difficult task of change. And so it came to be that I created a tool to assist me in managing through and overcoming my deficiencies—the Gueri Notes Process.

May 31, 2004, is when it all started. I knew enough about myself and my shortcomings to realize that I desperately needed structure if I was going to actually succeed at writing a different future.

I needed a companion. An accountability partner. Natalie had given me a notebook as a gift, but it had never been used. I threw it in my bag on the way out the door, opened it that morning at my desk, and began to write. First, I spent time journaling. I wrote about what I was proposing to do and what I hoped to accomplish, how I planned to get there and the results that I desired. Then, I made a list of things to do. I added to the list throughout the day and took copious notes in every exchange. The next morning I began again, writing about the successes of the previous day and setting a mindset for what was to come. I started a new list by rewriting the unfinished tasks from the day before, added new, and so it went. As I read and learned, I found myself wanting to capture the notes in that very same book. Before long, it was my trusted friend at work, church, home, meetings, lunch, classes . . . everywhere. There just seemed to be things to learn, and commitments to keep, wherever I went.

When I completed that first notebook and purchased another, I realized that what I had captured and created was worth saving and organizing for future reference. I reread the notebook, created a table of contents in the front cover, and added my most important lessons learned in the back. Then came books two, three, four . . . At the end of the first 90 days, I couldn't believe what I had accomplished, what I had learned, and how much I had grown. It seemed only fitting that I would reread and reflect. The exercise ingrained the lessons, and thus I made the decision to make it a priority every quarter.

After 12 months of disciplined use, religiously following the steps, I was amazed at the transformation that had occurred for me both personally and professionally. I was moved by the moment and proud of what I had done, but it didn't seem right for me to keep it all to myself. So, I dedicated time to reread and relive the whole year through my notebooks. As I read, I made a master list of lessons learned and shared it with friends, family, business associates, and, of course, kept a copy in my briefcase to be read again and again. Nearly 20 years later, I haven't changed a single thing to the process that began on that Monday morning in 2004, and I have rarely missed a day.

The journaling is therapeutic, inspiring, and clarifying and encourages deep thought and goal-oriented action. Fanatically managing a list of actionable items in a consistent system breeds responsibility, encourages delegation, and prioritizes one's most limited resource—time. Becoming a masterful notetaker, in one's own hand, stimulates the brain, requires focused attention, and captures the data for future use—a second brain. Rereading, reflecting and sharing drive the learnings deep into your mind and truly make you smarter. Best of all, the steps came in the form of a tool that brings them all together into a beautiful methodology for managing life.

The second challenge you gave me was to reread, refine and ultimately produce a list of the main principles that have come as a result of my years of learning and using this system. I had no idea just how challenging of a task this would be, but it took months of carving out small snippets of time to produce what came to be five principles. After years of use from the day I began the challenge, I had accumulated thousands of pages of notes from books, meetings, classrooms, experiences and conversations.

In those years, I had traveled the world, met with fascinating people, learned the value of a team of mentors (like you), and taken classes at incredible institutions like Harvard, University of Virginia, and the U.S. Army War College. I walked the beaches at Normandy with the Chief of Military History from West Point, read nearly 100 books on topics ranging from people to strategy, and the list goes on. I came to understand that my thirst for knowledge centers on a single theme: the desire to capture and grow from the wisdom and behaviors that make extraordinary people extraordinary. It was quite an emotional day when I completed the list of principles (Responsibility, Focus, Curiosity, Humility, Service), only to realize that the steps that I had been doing for years in my notebooks are guiding me on a lifelong journey to achieve these very principles. A virtuous cycle.

And that, my Friend, brings us full circle to the man that you have always known. More than two decades with this wonderful company, experiencing success and responsibilities that were unimaginable to the young man who sat down with a notebook in 2004. Best of all, 19 years of glorious marriage to the love of my life and three beautiful children. Now, there are five of us.

There is not a day that goes by that I don't thank God for the gift of Gueri Notes and the clarity of The Five Principles. But, it is you who inspired this project beyond a simple process for a single man. I have come to realize that the notebook I carry is a physical representation and a constant reminder of the commitment I made all of those years ago to break the cycle, to pursue extraordinary.

Life is precious. It is to be cherished. We are made to grow and to give all that we have to offer. We are in this together and we need each other. Now that it is finished, my hope is that this little book, the process, and the principles find their way to the one person who needs them most. May it serve them well on their mountain.

YOUR FRIEND
VERY TRULY ALWAYS,

Klint

Life is precious. It is to be cherished. We are made to grow and to give all that we have to offer. We are in this together and we need each other. Now that it is finished, my hope is that this little book, the process, and the principles find their way to the one person who needs them most. May it serve them well on their mountain.

THIS BOOK COMPRISES THREE THINGS:

THE PROCESS, THE PRINCIPLES,

AND THE PARTNERSHIP.

ONE

The Process

In all of my years of study, I have yet to meet or read about a successful person who did not have some type of system for organizing life. These systems vary wildly in their sophistication and complexity (from sticky notes to Cornell Notes), but it is abundantly clear to me that having a process for organizing each day, documenting and executing tasks, inspiring thoughtful time management, journaling, capturing wisdom, and sharing said wisdom with others is a foundational principle for pursuing excellence.

The Gueri Notes Process is the discipline that I lovingly share with you. There are five steps to Gueri Notes. You will find the process to be incredibly helpful in achieving higher levels of productivity, responsibility, and learning.

The process can be done with any type of notebook, legal pad, or stationery. However, I have created complementary Gueri Notebooks with the process built-in, should you find them helpful. As an aside, I spent years studying and experimenting with paper types, vellum covers, stitching for the binding, and tape for the spine. Even though I am a devotee of one type of pen, I tried them all—gel, roller, ballpoint, fountain, high-lighters, markers, and Sharpies—in an effort to ensure a great writing experience that will stand the test of time.

Regardless of whether you use the formal Gueri Notebook or the stationery you already have, the process itself is the most important part. The Gueri Notes Process is certainly not the only system out there worth pursuing, but I can tell you that this is a good one.

It works.

THE PROCESS

COMMIT TO USING THESE PRECISE STEPS. THE DEEPER THE CONNECTION TO THE PROCESS, AND THE MORE RIGID THE DISCIPLINE, THE GREATER THE OVERALL OUTCOME. AFTER 30 DAYS, DECIDE HOW BEST TO MOVE FORWARD, WITH GUERI NOTES IN ITS EXACT FORM OR YOUR OWN MODIFIED VERSION. EITHER WAY, HAVE A PROCESS FOR ORGANIZING LIFE THAT YOU ARE UNWAVERINGLY COMMITTED TO FOLLOW.

In every great novel or cinematic drama, there is a climactic moment when the pressure builds to a fever pitch and the protagonist must choose a path. We watch with nervous anticipation and hope that they choose the right way; the one that seems so obvious to us, the entertained. We know intuitively that if they choose right, we will be on our way to the happy and satisfying ending; glory abounds. Choose wrong and we are forced to live vicariously through the painful consequences of said choice; lessons learned. Life for us in the real world isn't all that different. Oftentimes the people around us see what we should do so clearly, and yet we regularly choose the way that comes with the painful consequences. "Easier said than done," as they say. And, unlike movies, life doesn't come with a tidy ending; credits roll and the pressure is over. Rather, we experience hundreds or even thousands of such "pivotal" moments in the entirety of our story.

May 31, 2004, was one such moment in time for me. A chaotic mess before. Choice presented. Decision made. A chaotic mess after, but, over time, through discipline, commitment, accountability and deep learning, things began to turn around. In an instant, through a single commitment to behavioral change, I reshaped the trajectory of my future. Thankfully, I got this one right and thus there seems no better place to begin than by sharing the very process that started it all on that day.

The incredible lesson that I stumbled into in my desperation and deep desire to change my present circumstances is a fact that is now quite evident to me but seemed so elusive at the time. People who have their "lives together," are dependable for others, and ultimately achieve a greater level of joy and success have a system for managing their life and all of the details that come with it. That system, which is personal and unique to all, provides a rhythm to life both personally and professionally. It is not an accident. They are not born with a greater sense of responsibility and ability (which is what I believed). They have made a choice and they execute.

For me, this was a revelation. It may be for you as well. It all begins here. If you do not have a clearly defined, disciplined methodology for managing life, this is a pivotal moment for you. Furthermore, if you choose not to read another chapter of this book, I want to implore you to read this one and commit either to using this system or to developing one for yourself. It is truly that important.

Gueri Notes, as I have come to call them, are the unchanged five steps that I referenced in the letter. The rhythm to life.

Begin each morning on a fresh page. Complete the date, page number and day of the week. Invest your first 15 minutes to journal; write, read, focus and think. A challenging time. A great memory. An idea. A hope for the day. Maybe a thought for the future, an "in hindsight" better way.

Next, list the things that are important for you to do. Extraordinary people accomplish their tasks and those that others ask them to. Look back at previous days and ensure that nothing is missed. Carry your notebook with you, ever prepared to add new to your list.

Take beautiful notes and record your life as art. Be curious. Be a learner and set yourself apart. Thoughtfully document every meeting, moment, book, meaningful conversation and class that you attend. Each day is full of lessons to learn and your education should never end.

Reread the notebook when it is finished and record your table of contents and most important lessons learned. Organizing your notes for reference and reflection is essential to transform knowledge into wisdom earned.

Reflect on the quarters as they close. The books for Q1, 2, 3 and 4. The exercise takes but a few minutes and increases your retention by many multiples or more. Celebrate the year by reading them all again. Document your most important lessons learned, carry them with you and share them with coworkers, family and friends.

As the chief user of this process over many years, I have learned much about why each step is important and how to get the most of the process. The balance of this chapter will dive into the "why" and "how" for using the Gueri Notes Process. Ultimately, though, the goal is not necessarily to carry these exact steps forward in life but rather to develop our own rhythmic habits that best complement our version of a pursuit of the extraordinary. If you are new to the idea of having a clearly established process for managing your life, then I want to encourage you to commit to using this exact process for the time it takes you to complete one notebook. This time spent executing the steps will give you a foundation from which you can build your own. No different than a celebrated musician, one must first spend time in study; learning to flawlessly execute the works of old masters in order to have the ability to then venture beyond the music to find one's own musical voice.

Begin each morning on a fresh page. Complete the date, page number and day of the week. Invest your first 15 minutes to journal; write, read, focus and think. A challenging time. A great memory. An idea. A hope for the day. Maybe a thought for the future, an "in hindsight" better way.

USING THE STEP:

Journaling is therapeutic. It clarifies your thoughts, documents your memories, and immortalizes moments for future reflection; good and bad. Making time to sit quietly and think intentionally about the issues you're facing, opportunities presented, or strategies worth considering will result in better, more thoughtful decision-making. The physical act of writing as you are thinking further deepens the cognitive experience. The exercises at the end of each principle in the coming chapters will provide thought-provoking questions to inspire your journaling. I call them "sparks of inspiration." Knowing what to journal about can be difficult for some at first. There really is no science here other than committing to the act for a sustained period will ultimately lead to your ability to easily sit and write. You will eventually know the topics intuitively, but I have provided a few thought starters and examples that I use when nothing obvious comes to mind:

- Read an inspirational or educational story, then write about what inspires you in the lesson.

  Keep books on the desk where you will most likely sit and journal. Inspirational titles, self-help books, business books, devotionals, books of quotes . . . anything that will speak to growth and change. Read a chapter or two until something catches your attention and write about it.

  Located in the back of this book is a list of some of my favorite quotes and lessons from my own years of study. Additionally, there is a list of 50 great books. Enjoy!

- Make a list of things in your life that you are grateful for and why.

  Watch my dear friend Shawn Achor's TED Talk, "The Happy Secret to Better Work." Shawn prescribes the writing of three gratitudes each day along with a wealth of other priceless exercises for finding true happiness. Shawn's books are just the type that should live on your desk to be read over and over again.

- Write about someone who has been impactful in your life (positively or negatively). Are there lessons to take from their example? If positive and possible, tell them about it.

  Write specifically to people even if you do not intend to share the words directly. But, of course, it's even better if you follow up that day's journaling about someone who has made a special, positive impact on your life by giving them a call or writing them a letter.

  Writing about the negative examples is equally important. Again, I have found that writing directly to that person is helpful in formulating your thoughts and maximizing the learning from the experience. Furthermore, if possible, this might serve as a catalyst to attempt to rectify the relationship or to explore how you might have also contributed to the negative outcome.

- Document meaningful moments: marriages, anniversaries, births, deaths, new jobs, promotions, demotions, etc. Always write about the emotions, the impact and the lessons.

  I love to think about people reading my notebooks 200 years from now just as I find such incredible value in reading people's words from the past. It will be fascinating to the reader in future generations just as it will be to you later in life, and your kids and grandchildren. Creating the ability to relive moments from life at a deeper level, joyous and tragic, is something you will cherish. It provides a perspective of growth and progress that is difficult to achieve in any other way.

- Write about behaviors you would like to see in yourself in the day(s) ahead or before an important meeting or event. How would you like to act or be received? What would you like to say or not say? What is the outcome you are hoping for?

Self-talk and visualization are things we do naturally. There are two types—positive and negative. Positive self-talk is what I am prescribing as we have a tendency to easily worry about all of the things that might go wrong. Rather, write about all of the things that you want to see go right and visualize their execution with pen and page.

Next, list the things that are important for you to do. Extraordinary people accomplish their tasks and those that others ask them to. Look back at previous days and ensure that nothing is missed. Carry your notebook with you, ever prepared to add new to your list.

USING THE STEP:

Carry your notebook wherever you go. Within reason, of course. Make it a habit to write everything down that needs to be done; at work and at home, things you feel you need to do and those that others need for you to do. Put personal and professional to-dos in the same list. There are no medals for memory, only execution, and the demands on your time from work and home should carry equal weight. The time you allocate to satisfy those tasks and the timing can vary, but they are all important nonetheless.

Prioritize your tasks and complete them in this order:

- For someone else (personal and professional)
- For the company (innovation, report review, learning trip, etc.)
- For me

Mark out the items as you complete them. Victory *is not* completing all of the items on your list each day. In fact, if you are regularly able to find the time to clear the entire list, there's a good chance that you can stretch yourself to accomplish more for yourself and for others. In this case, be actively seeking more personal or professional opportunities. Victory *is* making the absolute best use of every minute of your day executing the highest priority, biggest impact tasks for those relying on you and then for yourself. As you'll learn in the upcoming chapters on The Principles, extraordinary people are responsible and focused. This step is critical to accomplishing them both.

Make a new list every day referencing your previous day's list of unfinished items. Rewriting your unfinished tasks daily may seem like an unnecessary, almost silly use of your time, but the act itself is an important part of the process. For one, it forces you to go through a quick mental exercise that ensures you are making the best use of your time and are meeting the needs of others. As you rewrite unfinished items from the day before, ask these questions:

Is it still important?

- If the answer is "Yes," keep it. If "No," scratch it out and don't think about it again.
- The "Yes" items you have deemed important and will roll over every day until finished or until you deem them no longer important.

Am I procrastinating?

- If so, why and what can be done to eliminate this task?
- Procrastination does nothing but increase your stress and anxiety levels as well as the stress and anxiety for the affected parties.
- Watch the video by Brian Tracy called, "Eat That Frog!" A friend shared this simple, silly but incredibly impactful message with me years ago, and I am grateful for it.

Should this task (or can this task) be delegated?

- Delegation is critical to time management as well as building trust in teams and developing others.
- Make note of who you have transferred the item to and then scratch it from your list.
- Make a new task to follow up if necessary.

The second benefit of rewriting tasks daily and executing based on their priority is that the exercise gives you time to think before acting. Humans have a tendency (some more than others) to be infatuated with the new shiny penny. In this case, the shiny penny may be a "brilliant" idea or innovation that we are convinced will revolutionize our business, our people or our lives. Oftentimes, however, what seemed so "shiny" yesterday loses its luster over the coming days and weeks after you have given time for it to marinate in your mind. In this process you absolutely write down that new idea but you do not take action toward its development or implementation until its priority reaches the top . . . or you have attended to the truly more important things first. This balance helps you to be most effective with your time, your thinking, your priorities and those of your peers. It helps to prevent (notice I didn't say cures) you from being a leader who regularly sends people running down random rabbit holes (again, some of us more than others) as it elongates your thinking. Only the best ideas with real potential value earn meaningful resource allocation.

Third, the exercise encourages you to leverage the brains and energy of the talented men and women in your life. When you do have an idea worth dedicating resources to its exploration, empowering someone else to take the lead not only can result in a better outcome but plants seeds of growth, development, and trust within your team.

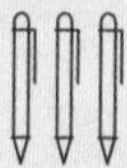

Take beautiful notes and record your life as art. Be curious. Be a learner and set yourself apart. Thoughtfully document every meeting, moment, book, meaningful conversation and class that you attend. Each day is full of lessons to learn and your education should never end.

USING THE STEP:

Take copious notes in every setting. Treat your notes like a historical record, one that you will return to in the future, as will future generations. Write as much as you feel is relevant and be thoughtful about your handwriting for later reference. This is a gift you are giving to your future self. You will come to love those old notes, and they will continue to teach you and others for years to come.

It is quite a shame to me that handwriting, particularly in cursive, seems to be a thing of the past. I propose that we seed the revolution that brings penmanship back!

Reread the notebook when it is finished and record your table of contents and most important lessons learned. Organizing your notes for reference and reflection is essential to transform knowledge into wisdom earned.

USING THE STEP:

Reread your notebook at its completion and fill out the table of contents in the front cover. You may not care to reference every single page or every day but rather just the important meetings, milestones, meaningful journal entries, lessons learned, etc. The moments that you know there is a chance you may want to revisit in a month, year, decade and you will be happy that it was noted for quick recovery.

As you read, make a special note of the lessons you learned in this chapter that really meant something to you; hit home, reshaped your worldview. Rewrite them on the Most Important Lessons Learned pages in the back.

Reflect on the quarters as they close. The books for Q1, 2, 3 and 4. The exercise takes but a few minutes and increases your retention by many multiples or more. Celebrate the year by reading them all again. Document your most important lessons learned, carry them with you and share them with your coworkers, family and friends.

USING THE STEP:

Make time every 90 days to reread your notebooks from the quarter. At the beginning of each year, reread the chapters you completed in the previous 12 months. The more time you take to reread and reflect, the more you drive learning and retention. Furthermore, the stories take on new life and the lessons new meaning. Reading them through a third, twelfth, or fiftieth time will spark new thoughts and actions to carry forward. They never get old.

You will find that you have learned so much and gained much wisdom. Make time to share your most important lessons learned with others.

i. Type them and send the list to a family member(s), a friend(s) or a coworker(s). Someone (or a group of people) who you feel would find value in learning what you've learned. –Or–

ii. Create a spreadsheet that you build upon each year. Note the author and create categories—business, personal growth, leadership, spirituality, etc. All of which will allow for sorting and quick recall. –Or–

iii. Send the year's lessons in a handwritten note. –Or–

iv. Invite someone to lunch and share your lessons learned over a meal and conversation. –Or–

v. Do all of the above. No matter what you choose, just share the wisdom with others. The exercise will be mutually beneficial.

The moral to the story of this first chapter is that extraordinary people have a rote system that they have created, borrowed, or built upon that roots them to the ground and keeps the engine of life moving forward. Not only is this a critical component to finding and maintaining success but it is also a requirement for maximizing the benefit of The Five Principles in the following chapters.

Writing this book has been two parts hobby and one part obsession inspired in 2012 by one of my dearest friends and mentors, Jim Denison, PhD. As you will learn in the upcoming chapter, Jim challenged me to do two things: 1) reproduce the rote process that has been so instrumental to me in achieving success in a way that it can be easily understood and replicated by others (the Gueri Notes Process) and 2) analyze the thousands of pages of notes that I have amassed over nearly two decades of study and condense them down to the critical few principles—the common threads that bind the whole. The net result of that multiyear research project is a list of five principles that I now see so clearly have served as the backbone for my personal journey of continuous improvement.

I will unpack each of the five, provide a deep dive into their background and meaning, and supply a handful of provocative questions (sparks of inspiration) and exercises to drive your journey and learning. The overarching goal is for all of the principles to become deeply embedded over the course of this project and subsequently to put a laser focus on one principle at a time in the days/weeks/months/years to come.

The Principles

THE FIVE PRINCIPLES

Preparing for The Five Principles

There are several ways to utilize the lessons and exercises provided in each chapter of The Five Principles.

- Read them through no differently than you would any other book, only digging in deeper when you find a subject to be particularly relevant to your life right now.
- Read a chapter a day, possibly during your journaling time, and work through the exercises in your Gueri Notebook or notebook of choice.
- Focus on one chapter a week for the next five weeks, again utilizing your journaling time to write about the lessons and exercises in your notebook.
- . . . One a month for the next five months . . .

–OR–

- My personal methodology is to live inside one chapter for the entire time that I am using a Gueri Notebook. It typically takes me about 45 days to use all of the pages in a Gueri Notebook, and I dedicate that single notebook to the act of self-disruption as it pertains to that single principle. There is a blank below the author line on the front cover of a Gueri Notebook. This is where I write the principle that each notebook is dedicated to disrupting. When I finish the notebook dedicated to "Service" (the fifth principle), I start again at "Responsibility." And, so it goes.

- Lastly, this is also a process that works really well in a small group setting with a mentor or mentee, Bible study, peer group, leadership team, etc. You will see when you get into the meat of each principle that certain parts require a tremendous amount of trust and vulnerability to be successful. Keep that in mind before venturing into this exercise with others. In fact, if you're the leader who is thinking about introducing this as a tool with your team or group, I recommend going through it first on your own before introducing the project to others. This will afford you the opportunity to properly gauge the appropriateness of its use or the proper strategy for utilization in your particular application.

Responsibility

Responsibility

1

EXTRAORDINARY PEOPLE ARE RESPONSIBLE PEOPLE. THEY DO NOT FORGET. THEY ARE ACCOUNTABLE. THEY CAN BE LEANED UPON BECAUSE THEY FORM A ROCK-SOLID FOUNDATION FOR THOSE AROUND THEM. THEIR MEMORY AND ACCOUNTABILITY ARE NOT NECESSARILY GENETIC, BUT RATHER HONED THROUGH PRACTICE. THEY HAVE A SYSTEM FOR GUARANTEEING THEIR RESPONSIBILITY AND ARE DILIGENT IN ITS USE.

Responsibility

When we were children, we dreamed big! Nothing was impossible, and we were unabashedly open about the scope of our dreams. No barriers existed between fantasy and reality. The thought of hurtling to the moon strapped to a rocket ship or stepping to the plate in the pivotal moment of a World Series baseball game was as real as the home you lived in and your family within it. We gave no thought to how we would get there. It was simply all going to be true . . . in due time.

Undoubtedly, none of us dreamed of, nor longed for, the day when we could count ourselves as a "responsible adult." The reality is we felt quite the contrary about the concept of responsibility. When we are young, the idea of being responsible is associated with the negative notions of growing older—oppressive, devoid of creativity, the death of spontaneity, boring. Is it not a beautiful thing about gaining some years and maturity that we now realize the people who actually become the astronaut or the baseball legend or simply live a life we wish to emulate earned that right by being highly responsible and disciplined people? Responsibility is not the death of the dream . . . It is the beginning!

All of us have men and women in our lives who we would easily categorize as a "rock" of responsibility. We admire them. We rely upon them, and one thing I have learned through my own personal experience is that they didn't earn that moniker overnight, but rather through many years of consistent dependability. The "rock" that sits easily at the top of my list is my grandfather, Hollis to many but Papa to me. Papa was more than just a grandfather. He was one of my best friends and my hero. Eleven at the time of the Great Depression, he grew up on a ranch in West Texas where challenges were expected, hard work was just work, and everyone played their part. He received his undergraduate degree at McMurry University in Abilene. A naval officer in World War II, he piloted a bomber called a Vega Ventura in the Pacific theater. After the war he returned to Texas to begin the next chapter of life with his beautiful wife, Lyda Lee, and (very shortly thereafter) their three children, one of whom was my mother. Papa was a high school agriculture teacher from then until the time of his retirement back to the country to tend to the family farm some 30 years later.

One of the stories about Papa that I admire the most, and is revelatory of this man and his character, was relayed to me by my grandmother when I was a young man. In the mid 1950s, money was tight for this family of five surviving on the single income of a small-town teacher. While they never went without a meal and hot water to bathe, there was certainly nothing left over at the end of the month—no room for error, a frightening position for children of the Depression. In the years immediately following the war, the American economy boomed. Military pilots were in high demand as the confluence of wartime technology and disposable income ushered in the dawn of commercial aviation. Mama, Lyda Lee, said the phone would ring at least once a week around dinnertime. The call was always for Papa, and it was always an airline offering to quadruple

Responsibility

his salary if he would come and fly. Each time he would listen politely, decline their offer, and return to the dinner table to quietly finish his supper.

Mama was not afraid to speak her mind, but she had so much love and respect for my grandfather that she didn't question his decisions. Save for one time, in a particularly weak moment, at a particularly difficult time for the family financially. "Daddy?" as she often called him, "Won't you at least take a meeting with those people? We are struggling here and flyin' for them might mean a better future for our children." Papa was a man of few words, so when he spoke it was always worth listening to, and this time was certainly no exception. According to Mama, he looked up from his plate and in his quiet, calm, yet authoritative tone said, "Mommy, if everybody chose their profession solely for the money, there wouldn't be anyone left to teach our children. That doesn't sound too good to me for their future." With that, he went back to chewing.

The Papa I knew was a rancher, up at five every morning to make coffee and to deliver a cup to my grandmother while she slept "a few extra minutes." A hearty breakfast fueled the morning's responsibilities, feeding the cows and tending to the upkeep of the ranch. Back home for lunch, a nap, and then more work until dinner. Every evening was capped off by falling asleep in the recliner to the evening news only to be awoken by the sound of "The Star-Spangled Banner" as the station signed off at midnight. He made sure his family never missed a Sunday church service, gave generously to the community with his time and his resources, and was the kind of man who would drop everything to help a neighbor catch a loose bull, or drive for three hours to make his grandson's baseball game.

Papa was a "rock" because he took care of his responsibilities, lived well within his means, knew his purpose and was committed to it, and was always there when you needed him most. His unwillingness to procrastinate allowed him always to be prepared to help when called. He was physically fit and mentally and spiritually healthy, and he had a system for managing the demands of life and the needs of others. Although far less complicated than the Gueri Notes Process, Papa's system worked for him. His consisted of a calendar and a spiral notebook. The calendar was the kind that he received from his insurance agent each year with the puffy red plastic top. He stuck it to the dash in his truck. Important dates were circled and notated; finished months were never removed so as to make the transfer of dates to next year's calendar simple. His spiral notebook sat on top of his dirt-road-dusty dashboard. He jotted down notes on herds, crops, feed, mileage and anything else noteworthy. It all worked because he was disciplined.

The list of lessons learned from Papa is long, but the one that stands tallest is that *being responsible is a choice.*

To achieve your maximum influence, you must first be dependable and responsible. Said another way, your ship needs to be in order before you can help someone else with their ship. Let

Responsibility

alone a fleet of ships. Papa also taught me that living responsibly goes well beyond an effective ability to execute tasks. Healthy disciplines in the categories of finance, health and wellness, and personal relationships should carry equal weight to professional pursuits. Truly responsible people are physically fit, mentally capable, financially stable, and spiritually/emotionally healthy. Each of the buckets requires its own plan and constant maintenance.

It is not the path of least resistance and takes tireless work, the ability and the inspiration to make difficult choices, and the discipline to maintain positive habits. Responsibility is not the easy way, but the effort is worth the outcome.

Papa wasn't a CEO or a multimillionaire. He didn't climb the ranks at a corporation or a law firm, but yet he was one of the most successful, competent, and capable men that I have ever known. We would all be so lucky to be counted as a "rock" like Papa.

One of history's most legendarily responsible men was none other than the original commander in chief, George Washington. Whether or not a history buff, all are familiar with the famous virtues of the man from Mount Vernon. And there's much to know about his character beyond the fictitious story of the cherry tree. Fanatical about order and fueled by discipline, General Washington took care of his image of responsibility and believed deeply in adhering to routine for success. He was always conscious of his need to remain healthy in order to be available for those in his care. He knew his limits with alcohol, abhorring drunkenness. He was fastidious with his clothing and made it a point to never be seen publicly without being dressed and quaffed to exacting standards. His air was one of calm confidence in the face of any situation or danger. His consistent behavior inspired his men and lent comfort in the most dire of situations. Beyond all others, though, my favorite fact about the exemplary life of George Washington as an example is the fact that he was a master journal writer and notetaker. Never without his notebooks, Washington documented everything; from the mundane figures regarding crops and livestock to the deep and sentimental reflections from a man tested to the extremes of human endurance. The practice undoubtedly assisted in his uncanny ability to recall specific facts about situations, maintain balance and order in life, and provide a working document by which he grew from and developed wisdom through his remarkable life experiences. George Washington was extraordinary.

One of my favorite true stories about Washington occurred after the British fell at Yorktown but before the final outcome of the negotiated peace treaty in Paris officially ended the Revolutionary War. Washington, conscious of the historical value of his wartime documents, had them carted under armed guard in a caravan back to Virginia. He may have loved his notebooks just as much as I do.

Responsibility

Living responsibly is the sum of the myriad tiny choices that we make each day. These often small, seemingly inconsequential decisions build upon each other, one by one, culminating in transformative behaviors and evolutionary change. The kid in you recoils from the fact that these choices are often the difficult, uncomfortable ones that deep down we know we should make but either choose to ignore, loom too large to conquer, or are simply too lazy or lack the self-awareness to tackle. It takes discipline and delayed gratification to shape ourselves into a person who others would count as responsible. And, shoring up our foundation and reshaping the way we think about how we spend our time, talents and resources are the critical first steps to giving ourselves every opportunity to realize our greatest potential.

This book serves as the jump start, accountability partner or spark of inspiration to do the things that we often already know we should do. We are committing to the arduous work of radical self-disruption for the purpose of shaping ourselves into a person who achieves the extraordinary.

In this chapter, we will first create a disciplined rhythm to approaching each day. Start small. Just following the five steps of the Gueri Notes Process outlined in Chapter 1 will result in positive change and growth to celebrate. But, as we begin to feel the disciplined process taking hold, we should take the opportunity to dive deep into the various categories of our lives and assess our strengths and weaknesses; successes and failures.

The sparks of inspiration that follow are not prescriptive, but are rather there to provide some guidance and suggestions on exercises to do and/or areas to investigate. No one knows you better than you; stay within the lines or color completely off the page. It's up to you.

1. journaling for 15 minutes in the morning
2. making a detailed list of tasks / adding to throughout the day / deliberate time management / execution
3. taking copious notes in all settings
4. reflecting / rereading / deep learning / wisdom-building retention
5. pouring into the lives of others through sharing said wisdom

When we live intentionally to take care of ourselves, our business, and the needs of those around us in a responsible way, we actually put ourselves in the best possible position to take the most joy from life.

Responsibility provides the freedom for us to fully live.

WARM-UP WRITING

- When you were a child, what did you dream to be as a grown-up? Write that story.
- Did your dreams come true? Why or why not?
- If your dreams didn't work out as planned, do you see any parallels in what you do now that link to the passions you had as a child? Do you have opportunities to fulfill those passions in other ways?

WRITE ABOUT THE MOST RESPONSIBLE, DEPENDABLE PEOPLE IN YOUR LIFE. WHO'S YOUR "PAPA"?

- Interview them if it's still possible or if you (and they) can make the time.
- What are the traits and behaviors that made them someone who achieved the highest levels of responsibility?
- Why do you admire them?
- What can you learn from them and adapt to your own life?
- Be open and vulnerable about your own challenges and seek their wise counsel.

CONSIDER AND REFLECT UPON THE CATEGORIES OF YOUR LIFE.

Make time to analyze each and think about what it means to be truly responsible in each area. Identify your deficiencies. Plan for what success looks like and strategize on ways to implement new behaviors and habits to achieve your goals. Use your first 15 minutes each day to journal, think, and hold yourself accountable.

Responsibility

Personal Life/Relationships

- Ask yourself what the opportunities you can easily identify are.
- Time management—professional vs. personal.
- Screen time vs. face time (not the Apple version but actually looking at someone's face, in person, and listening to them and responding). Are you present when you're present?
- Ask others. Make time to have intentional conversations with your spouse or significant other, friends, family members. Ask them if they view you as a responsible person in each of the various categories and seek their counsel on ways they would like to see you improve.
- Identify behaviors that will help create change (e.g., turn off the phone when you're home, change clothes when you walk in the door so you can play with the kids).

Professional Life/Career

- What does being truly responsible in your workplace look like?
- What are the opportunities for you to improve?
- What things can you do or behaviors can you change that would help?

Health and Wellness

- Do you know the true state of your health?
- When was the last time you went to the doctor for a full physical? Is it time?
- What is your plan for regular exercise?
- How do you maintain a healthy diet?
- Any destructive habits that need to be addressed? What's your plan?

Personal Finances

- When was the last time that you checked your credit?
- Are there plans for fixing/improving if necessary?
- Do you have at least six months of savings? If not, what is your strategy for making the necessary adjustments to your expenses and standard of living in order to do so?
- Do you give? Consider the importance of a healthy discipline of saving AND giving.

Responsibility

Spiritual Life/Emotional Well-Being

- Do you feel spiritually/emotionally healthy?
- Everyone needs a trusted source to talk to and strategize with at all stages of life; good and bad. Do you have that someone? When was the last time you visited with them?
- Are you connected to a community; personal, spiritual, and/or professional?
- Do you give of your time?

Disciplined living, intentional listening and predictable action characterize a responsible person. This chapter challenges you to think honestly about how well you perform in these categories and to make the appropriate adjustments in the spirit of continuous improvement. Papa passed away long ago, but there's certainly not a day that goes by that I don't think of him, his impact on me, his example as a "rock." I dedicate this principle in his honor, and I implore you to dedicate this time of reflection, learning and growth in honor of that special somebody that is your version of Papa.

USE YOUR GUERI NOTEBOOK COMPANION OR YOUR OWN NOTEBOOK TO JOURNAL ON THESE QUESTIONS ABOUT YOUR LIFE—PERSONAL, PROFESSIONAL, AND SPIRITUAL.

If you are not already, you will someday be the "rock" for another. I can think of no greater honor or responsibility.

Focus

PRINCIPLE TWO

Focus

2

EXTRAORDINARY PEOPLE HAVE
A DESTINATION IN MIND. THEY
HAVE A PLAN. BOTH PATIENT AND
PERSISTENT, THEY PRESS ON EACH DAY
TO MASTER THEIR CRAFT. ON THEIR
JOURNEY, ACHIEVED GOALS LIE BEHIND
THEM AND WORTHY GOALS LIE AHEAD.

Focus

Our patience withers as technology advances. We have grown accustomed to the ability to satisfy our desires for most things nearly instantaneously. This demand for "on-demand" is a mostly positive evolution when discussing goods and services, communication or transportation, but can be quite destructive in the realms of personal, professional and intellectual development. In such cases, expecting maturity or fulfillment without the time, repetition and focus needed for mastery and overcoming adversity will mainly deliver disappointment.

Our world is changing so rapidly that it's nearly impossible not to get swept up in its current. This constant evolution of the way we shop, chat, earn a living and travel can make us feel as though something is wrong with us if we, too, are not going through some major change in our lives. It seems that as a people we are losing our ability and our appreciation for the importance of being selectively and intentionally patient, to focus and make commitments. It is simply too easy to rearrange our lives when experiencing the slightest discomfort. The truly tragic potential byproduct of our collective impatience is that most of the really special things in life that we can have, accomplish, create or learn cannot be achieved overnight nor can they be obtained without some form of discomfort. We are stunting our growth and extinguishing the opportunities for meaningful, wisdom-building experiences.

We need not go back too far in history to see the evolution clearly. When the GIs returned home from WWII, they found work in the freshly booming, postwar economy. These battle-hardened young men were grateful to have employment, stability, steady pay, and the opportunity to provide for their new families. Not to mention the fact that they were happy to report to a factory or an office over a foxhole. Their desire was to work hard and, with a little luck and good performance, over time they would hope to see their careers grow. It was not uncommon at all for these men to spend the next 40 years at the same company, or in the same field. Ultimately, through time and repetition, they became masters at their craft.

With each subsequent generation, thanks in large part to peace and prosperity, the total number of professions, industries and/or companies that one works for in their most productive years has multiplied many times over. And, as a result, our mental state has shifted when beginning a new job from permanence to non-permanence; from being mentally permanent like our grandfathers (or great-grandfathers) to a state of being mentally temporary. Think about it this way: when more recent generations start a new job, they tend to enter into that commitment for "the time being" or "until something better comes along" or "until I find my passion." From the company's perspective, they are a permanent employee, but from the employee's perspective, the company is temporary. Clearly, odds are they won't build a lifelong career in the very first job they accept, but the slight difference in the mental state with which they begin can have a dramatic impact on whether or not they actually find the type

Focus

of success that might lead to a long-term, fruitful career at that company or in that industry.

We can all agree that there is no such thing as a perfect job. Even the most successful organizations with a celebrated culture, development potential, continuing education, great pay and great benefits have their struggles. When we work at that great company in a temporary mental state, the people we don't like or processes that annoy us go on the unconscious list we keep of the things we hope to solve in the search for our next job. However, when we work in that same environment and are mentally permanent (even for a fixed amount of time, i.e. two, three, five years, but defined nonetheless), that same list is transformed into relationships to work through or mend, and processes to accept or influence. Again, slight difference, but a world apart in opportunity and outcome.

To illustrate this point, imagine for a moment that you were *offered* an opportunity to live in a home for the next five years. The rent is a fraction of the cost of other comparable properties in the area and it's an easy walk to work. You are welcome to break the agreement at anytime with no negative financial consequences. The only catch is that you cannot tour the property in advance. Clearly, you go into this situation very optimistically and are excited at the prospect of saving money and walking to work. Surely, how bad can it be? Moving day is the first time that you are allowed to see your new home, and you are shocked and dismayed when you walk in the door to find that it is an absolute dump! All phases of emotion flood over you, but ultimately you resign to give it a try considering the financial benefit and the commute. Despite your best efforts, the fact that you know that you can walk away at anytime gnaws at you morning, noon and night. What are the odds that you see it through? Probably very, very low.

Conversely, you are given this same scenario with one minor difference. This time you are *required* to live in the home for five years. You cannot break this contract. You make a commitment. When you walk in the door on moving day, you experience the same emotional roller coaster, but (I contend) an entirely different outcome. Once resigned to the fact that the circumstances are what they are for the next 60 months, you go straight to work to clean up the house and make modest improvements. Same home. Same person. Different mindset. The removal of the easy escape plan sets you up for finding a way to successfully navigate the unexpected and maximize the benefits of the opportunity.

In the first chapter, Responsibility, we exercised focus by clearly identifying areas in our life that needed improvement for the sake of building a strong foundation from which we can grow. Chapter 2, Focus, encourages us to dream big about what we hope to build upon that foundation. The exercises will help us identify the areas in our life where we owe it to ourselves and others to shift into a permanent mental state; to focus and commit. This focus doesn't just have to be related to work but

Focus

can be many things, across every aspect of our life—learning to play an instrument, writing a book, finishing college, planning for retirement. It also doesn't have to span for 40 years like our grandfathers but is much more about becoming aware, making plans, setting time-bound goals, being patient and staying focused.

The type of focus that we hope to achieve is holistic, life-shaping, meaningful. Short-term and long-term goals are critical to build the momentum necessary for reaching a desired destination. But, one must first understand where they are going and for what purpose in order to chart their course.

Pick up just about any biography on someone who has accomplished something truly extraordinary in life, and you will find a story of intense, almost superhuman focus. A deep understanding of one's noble purpose and an unwavering commitment to see it through is a central characteristic of those who change the world or reshape history. Consider Abraham Lincoln. Few men have lived who were more obviously knitted for a specific moment in history than President Lincoln. Inaugurated as our nation's sixteenth president at the precise moment when the country appeared on the precipice of destruction, Lincoln's resolve to preserve the union at all costs is the reason that the United States remains the symbol of freedom and democracy for the world today. Abraham Lincoln sacrificed all, literally, in the pursuit of his goal.

Thankfully, not all of us were created to shepherd a civil war, and it is clearly an extreme example, but it is no less important for us to learn the lesson. There are times in our lives when our circumstances dictate our focus, and there are times when it is in our best interests to force ourselves into focus. The person who not only changed the trajectory of my life through the lesson of focus but has also modeled a focused life for me to aspire to is, again, Dr. Jim Denison, one of my mentors.

It was Dr. D, as I affectionately refer to him, who sat with me in the airport in Washington, DC, all of those years ago and challenged me to do this work. Our relationship began in 2002 when a mutual friend thought that I would benefit from spending time with him. In hindsight, I have absolutely no idea why he agreed to meet me for breakfast other than out of obligation to his friend and that he is just that kind. I was 23 years old and struggling mightily, and Dr. Denison was an incredibly accomplished and successful pastor of a 10,000-member church in Dallas. A church, I must add, of which I was not a member.

Today, Jim is the focused chief vision officer for Denison Ministries and the co-founder of the Denison Forum on Truth and Culture. The organization that bears his name is dedicated to the continuation of his noble purpose; to leverage his gifts and the gifts of those around him to speak and write truth on cultural and contemporary issues. To help a normal person like me to better understand events as they unfold in our world, what they mean, why I should care, and how they affect me and my family.

Focus

Dr. D is uniquely suited to tackle, unpack, dissect, and make sense of the most difficult of topics. Precisely the kinds of topics that others avoid. He wakes at 4:00 a.m. daily, no matter where he is, to produce *The Daily Article*, a column that is distributed by email to more than 340,000 readers around the globe with the podcast being downloaded more than 70,000 times every month. Dr. Denison's social media following is over 2.2 million with 400,000-plus followers on Facebook. He runs a successful organization, serves on countless boards, and speaks around the world on topics such as medical ethics, genetic medicine, reproductive science, geopolitics, and religious liberties, just to name a few. Somehow he finds time to teach doctoral seminars, preaches most Sundays, and has written 20 books, so far.

Dr. Denison is the kind of person that you cannot help but stand in awe of his accomplishments and wonder how he could possibly find the time or the energy. It is clear that he possesses a tremendous amount of natural skill and a superhero ability to function with very little sleep, but above all he is focused. Jim is acutely aware of his noble purpose. He sets audacious goals in the pursuit of fulfilling that purpose and breaks down the big into myriad small, manageable goals that over time build the whole. He is great at saying "no." When he is working toward something specific, he is thoughtful about avoiding distractions (even things he would enjoy or have value) in order to remain steadfast in his efforts. Jim has learned to make every minute count.

It is difficult to quantify the impact that Jim has had on my life and the countless lives around the world, but I will close this chapter with a specific lesson that he taught me about focus. I went to work for the company that I still work for to this day in 2001. It was a great job right from the start with wonderful people, admirable values and tremendous opportunity. Despite this, 18 months into the job, at the peak of my success up to that point, I became distracted by another opportunity and left. There's no need for the dirty details of the next 10 months just to say that it was an unmitigated disaster. Right back to square one . . . maybe even a bit further.

It was during this time that I met with Jim to seek his counsel, and he gave me another provocative challenge that set success in motion. Dr. D challenged me to commit to returning to the company and staying put, in whatever capacity they needed, for five years. By establishing the challenge to commit for five years, no matter what, he forced me to take meaningful steps in an effort to silence the voices in my head that relentlessly urged me to move on when stability began to bore.

It truly was a challenge, but it is one of the moments in time that, now looking back, changed everything. Fortunately, I was able to return to my previous employer in the same job (even the same office), but I was a wildly different person thanks to the focused commitment. I put the date five years into the future on my calendar. When that day arrived, I would allow myself the opportunity to reflect and decide if I would continue with

Focus

the company. Until then, I would just go to work. The big hairy audacious goal (B.H.A.G.) of surviving in the same role for such an amazing amount of time forced me to strategize on ways to change my behavior. But, it wasn't just the daily disciplines that changed; it was also my attitude. When you're committed to being in the same place with the same people doing the same job for five years, the way you treat people changes. I was nice before I left, but I was kind, caring and generous when I returned. Not only with the people I worked with but also with customers. There was suddenly an opportunity to build a meaningful relationship that transcended a single transaction. My entire outlook changed, and thusly so did everything else.

Needless to say more than two decades later and with professional joy and successes that were unimaginable to me then, I am forever grateful for his sage advice.

Find. Focus. Commit. Be patient and persistent. Repeat. Magic.

SPARKS OF

INSPIRATION

THOUGHTS ON HOW TO
EFFECTIVELY USE THIS CHAPTER

WARM-UP WRITING

- I believe that each of us is uniquely created for a specific purpose or purposes. What do you believe you were knitted for?

COMMIT TO USING THE FIVE STEPS OF THE PROCESS EACH DAY.

Begin the morning with a minimum of 15 minutes spent journaling; at home or at the office. Use the sparks of inspiration to inspire your writing and to create relevant tasks that impact behavior.

START SMALL. WHERE DO YOU KNOW THAT YOU LACK FOCUS OR COMMITMENT TODAY?

- Is it in the company you work for today (like the example story)?
- Are there particular areas in your work or home life that need your focus?
- Is there an area of your business where you are weak that you need to take the time to become more educated or more involved in?
- Is there something in your personal life that requires your attention—your marriage, your relationship with your children?

Focus

- Interview them if possible and if you (and they) can make the time.
- How did they determine that they had a noble purpose worthy of such commitment?
- When they became impatient or distracted along the way, how did they bring themselves back to focus?
- What can you learn from them and adapt to your own life?

GO BIG! WHAT ARE THE THINGS THAT YOU REALLY WANT TO ACCOMPLISH IN LIFE?

It may seem a bit cliché and a tad macabre, but a great exercise for encouraging the type of deep thinking that is required to establish a noble purpose for life is to write your own obituary. Give testimony to the life you lived, the accomplishments you achieved, the impact that you had on the world both personally and professionally. What is your legacy?

USING THE KNOWLEDGE YOU HAVE GAINED FROM THE PREVIOUS EXERCISES, WHAT COMMITMENTS DO YOU NEED TO MAKE IN ORDER TO TURN THOSE DREAMS INTO A REALITY?

As an example, you might commit to working for a particular company for five years, to going back to school to finish a degree or earn a new one, or to taking piano lessons for two years. Whatever you decide, put the date(s) on the calendar when your commitment expires and reflect and celebrate when the day arrives. Intentionally move from temporary to mental permanence.

WHAT ARE THE SHORT-TERM GOALS THAT NEED TO BE ESTABLISHED IN SUPPORT OF YOUR LONG-TERM COMMITMENT?

- Use your daily to-do list to force the execution of tasks and behaviors that will help you build and keep momentum.
- Use Peter Drucker's SMART goals methodology: Specific, Measurable, Achievable, Relevant, Time-Bound.

Focus

IN WHAT WAYS ARE YOU SPENDING TIME OR LOSING FOCUS TO THINGS THAT ARE MISALIGNED WITH YOUR NOBLE PURPOSE?

What do you need to learn to say "no" to?

All of us have a unique purpose, special skills, and much to offer. Use the Focus chapter to understand your contribution and to inspire you on the journey to making that supreme impact.

Curiosity

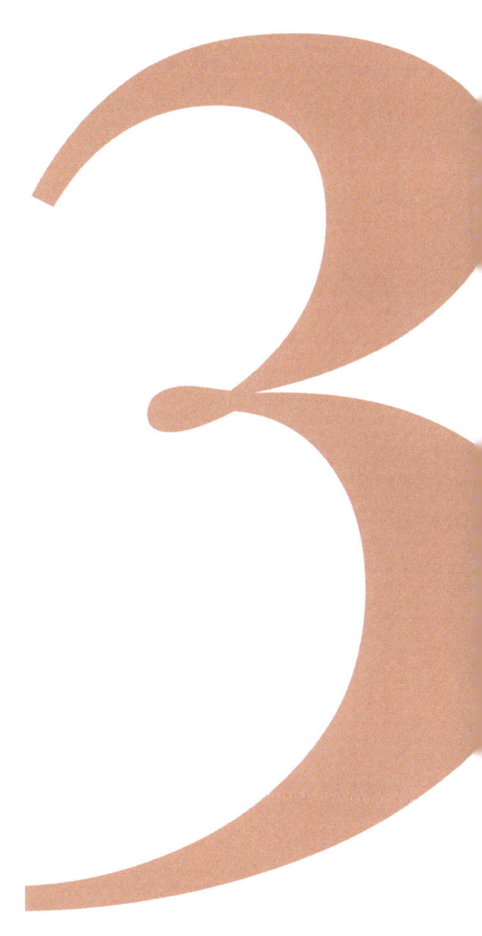

Curiosity

3

EXTRAORDINARY PEOPLE FIND THE ORDINARY EXTRAORDINARY. THERE ARE NO UNINTERESTING THINGS, JUST UNINTERESTED PEOPLE. CURIOSITY IS AN INSATIABLE DESIRE TO LEARN. THEY READ VORACIOUSLY. THEY HAVE MENTORS AND MENTOR OTHERS. THEY LISTEN AND ASK QUESTIONS. THEY HAVE MORE QUESTIONS THAN ANSWERS. THEY DON'T RUSH TO JUDGMENT BUT CAREFULLY CONSIDER. FOR THEM, IGNORANCE IS NOT AN EXCUSE BUT RATHER AN INVIGORATING OPPORTUNITY TO GROW.

Curiosity

One of the greatest gifts that we can give ourselves is a healthy discipline of continuous learning. The brain is a human's most valuable organ. No different than the 600 odd others in our body, the brain can and will atrophy with prolonged abuse or neglect. Intellectual stimulation is the mind's equivalent of a push-up. The exercise is similarly challenging, almost painful at times, but results in growth, speed, vigor and advantage. A sharp mind and an extensive education serve as competitive assets. Best of all, anyone can obtain such qualities. No specialized equipment required.

Leonardo da Vinci was one of mankind's greatest learners. His seemingly insatiable curiosity caused him to find wisdom and beauty in the unlikeliest of places. His fascination with dissecting (sometimes literally) to understand the how and why resulted in some of the world's greatest discoveries, engineering marvels centuries ahead of their time, and artistic masterpieces. But, the most priceless of gifts left to us by this remarkable man was not the *Mona Lisa* nor his inviable collection of notebooks. What we can take most from his example is a disciplined desire to learn and explore constantly. And, thus, to be permanently enriched by the smallest, seemingly inconsequential details in our everyday lives. Da Vinci's brilliance was found not in a God-given mind that we could never possess, but rather in his ability to slow down and study.

Chapter 1, Responsibility, helped to reshape our worldview into an understanding of the importance of setting a foundation of responsible, disciplined living. Chapter 2, Focus, helped us to explore our dreams, make plans, make commitments, and move from a temporary mental state to a permanent one. Chapter 3, Curiosity, helps us to recognize that our education shouldn't end after high school or college, but is just as important to our health and happiness and the achievement of our dreams as a healthy diet and regular exercise. Our goal in this chapter is to begin by learning how to learn and then to develop a life-long discipline for continuous improvement that we can carry forward in our lives.

Many years ago, I had the great privilege of participating in a leadership learning curriculum at the U.S. Army War College. It was a remarkable experience in a surreal setting. My class-mates were wildly accomplished men and women from various industries around the country and the subject matter was fas-cinating. I will never forget my time there nor will I forget the lessons that I learned. However, the whole experience pales in comparison to the friendship that was born as a result of those days at the Carlisle Barracks. It is how I got to know an amazing man named Colonel Cole Kingseed.

Interestingly though, the colonel wasn't present in Pennsylvania. Nor did he know that the class was even taking place. A fellow student mentioned over lunch one day that she knew a man that I would "really enjoy getting to know." She said that we are both great lovers of military history and we would "have fun visiting." She scribbled "Cole" and a phone number on a

Curiosity

piece of paper and made me promise that I would give him a call. Little did I know that the phone call would have such a profound impact.

The man on the other end of that phone line, the one I called out of obligation, was a 30-year veteran of the United States Army. A man who holds Master of Arts and doctorate degrees from the Ohio State University, and a Master of Arts in National Security and Strategic Studies from the U.S. Naval War College. A man who has authored six books, one of which, *Beyond Band of Brothers: The War Memoirs of Major Dick Winters*, was a *New York Times* bestseller. And last but certainly not least, a man whose military career culminated in his tenure as Full Professor of History and Chief of Military History at West Point.

It is still hard for me to believe that I have a friend like Cole. Much like Papa and Dr. D from the previous chapters, Cole is a man who possesses each of The Five Principles expressed in this project. But, the greatest gift that Col. Cole has imparted on me is an insatiable desire to learn—anything about anything and into perpetuity. One could easily discern that Cole is a learner just by reading his title, Colonel Cole Kingseed, PhD. A person doesn't get those three little letters at the end of their name without being dedicated to learning, but that's not the kind of desire to learn that I gained by being around Cole. He taught me the value of curiosity.

Over the years that I have known Cole, we have traveled together to extraordinary places and have created priceless memories. We have had countless conversations on the phone and by email. All the while I have been carefully observing him, listening, and taking notes. From my own notebooks, here are the lessons about curiosity that I have gleaned from my time with the colonel:

Read often. Read broadly. If you are not a reader, it is imperative that you make every effort to become one. Spend any time studying extraordinary people and it will be difficult to find one who doesn't credit reading as one of the secrets to their success. They read often and broadly.

"A reader lives a thousand lives before he dies. The man who never reads lives only one." GEORGE R. R. MARTIN

Curiosity

For some, reading is naturally enjoyable, and for others, the thought triggers painful memories of junior high stresses and desperate efforts to get your hands on CliffsNotes. For those of us whose educational development was stunted in the eighth grade, reading is a skill to be developed in adulthood rather than adolescence. We can do this. Start small and with a subject matter you are sure to enjoy. Don't be afraid to leverage your first 15 minutes of journaling time in this chapter to read and take notes. No different than an athlete's discipline for working out, make this a priority and commit the time to develop a routine and subsequently a habit.

Ten pages a day x five days a week x 52 weeks in a year = 2,600 pages / the average paperback book has 250 pages = 10 books every single year. This certainly doesn't sound like an insurmountable task. It requires effort and discipline.

We can have a robust debate on the value of audiobooks versus reading the old-fashioned way. Some view it as a dollar-for-dollar exchange, and others contend that reading rather than listening has a different impact on your mind and your ability to retain. For them, the preference is reading the old-fashioned way. However, in my opinion, audiobooks and podcasts are a wonderful innovation and are undoubtedly a better mechanism for learning than doing nothing at all. If it works for you, do it!

Reading to broaden knowledge in your career field, hobby interests, self-help, and personal development is just smart. But, it is equally important for you to read well outside of your comfort zone. Learning about industries unrelated to your own and subject matter outside of your interests and being exposed to different cultures and beliefs are wonderful ways to spark innovation and challenge your worldview. Furthermore, building deep and meaningful connections with other humans is of paramount importance to your ability to succeed and influence. The more broadly you read, the more likely you are to find common ground with others regardless of background, ethnicity, or field of work.

Remember, the point of reading is to be entertained, to learn, and hopefully both. If the primary goal is to learn, take your time and take notes. In either case, don't be afraid to give yourself permission to skip a chapter or two, or three, or even an entire book if you don't feel like you are growing as a result of the effort. Pick up something new. No one is keeping count, and getting stuck on a book that adds no value is a sure way to derail your progress.

HAVE MENTORS.

One of the greatest ways to build wisdom is to spend time with and learn from extraordinary people further down the road than you. Be intentional in your selection. Aim high. Try to find one for your personal life and one for your professional life. Who is someone that you see value in learning from their successes and their behaviors? Meet with them at least once every 90 days. Be prepared. Ask questions. Invite them to come

Curiosity

see your work. If possible, invite yourself to go see theirs. It is your responsibility as the mentee to drive the relationship, the agenda and the learning.

Colonel Cole's mentor for more than 20 years was none other than the famous World War II hero Major Dick Winters. If you are unfamiliar with Major Winters, watch the HBO miniseries *Band of Brothers,* produced by Tom Hanks and Steven Spielberg. You will not be disappointed.

That relationship not only spawned a lifelong friendship and countless hours of conversation, advice, and wisdom for the two men, but it also resulted in Cole's bestselling book, *Beyond Band of Brothers.*

MENTOR OTHERS.

Teaching someone else is one of the greatest ways that a person can stay sharp, focused, and striving for continuous improvement in their own life. Articulate and teach them the behaviors necessary for success and then hold yourself to that aspirational standard. There is great joy in sharing and helping someone else realize their greatest potential.

This chapter is dedicated to inspiring the curious life. During the time spent with this notebook, work to establish and maintain a healthy habit of continuous learning. You cannot possibly live long enough to learn everything that you would like. But, you should try. Let that knowledge open your eyes to the world of wisdom that is all around you. Be aware and be intentional.

Thirst for knowledge. Have your notebook with you, ever prepared to capture the wisdom as it comes.

THOUGHTS ON HOW TO EFFECTIVELY USE THIS CHAPTER

WARM-UP WRITING

- What is your favorite book or list of books? If you're not a reader yet, ask someone who you trust to make recommendations to get you started.
- P.S. I included a list of 50 Great Books in the last section of this book. Enjoy!

READ OFTEN. READ BROADLY.

- At a minimum, use your 15 minutes of journal time in this chapter to read.
- Take notes and build a habit.
- Pick up a book that is outside of your comfort zone.
- Join a book club or create your own. A book club is as simple as buying two copies and giving one to a friend, family member or coworker. Meet to discuss every few chapters.
- Make it a part of your normal routine to ask others for book recommendations.

SUBSCRIBE TO AND LEARN FROM PODCASTS.

- Ask your friends, family members, or coworkers for suggestions.
- Let this be supplemental learning that stretches and opens your worldview.

Curiosity

WHO IS YOUR MENTOR AND WHY?

- Be very thoughtful about who you target as a potential mentor.
- Find a mentor for your career and one for your personal life.
- Think deeply about the characteristics, behaviors, or qualities that you would aspire to emulate.
- They must be just as excited about mentoring you as you are about having them as a mentor. You should formally ask them so that they clearly understand your intent for the relationship.
- The mentee must drive the relationship, set the meetings, and come prepared with questions, challenges, and topics to discuss.
- Meet at least once every 90 days and communicate regularly.
- Write about them. What's their story? Why do you admire them? What can you learn from them? What have you learned from them?
- Ask your mentor for book recommendations. Read them.
- Read a book along with your mentor to discuss at your quarterly meetings.

MENTOR OTHERS.

- Who can you mentor?
- Complete *A Guide to Self-Disruption* along with your mentee.
- Use the overview from the previous question in reverse when thinking about who to mentor and how.

Humility

Humility

4

EXTRAORDINARY PEOPLE HUMBLY ACKNOWLEDGE THEIR STRENGTHS AND PERSISTENTLY IMPROVE THEIR WEAKNESSES. THEY WELCOME FEEDBACK WITHOUT DEFENDING THEIR EGO. THEY LEVERAGE THEIR STRENGTHS WITH HUMILITY. WEAKNESSES FUNCTION AS OPPORTUNITIES FOR PERSONAL DEVELOPMENT AND ACKNOWLEDGING WHERE OTHERS POSSESS STRENGTH.

Humility

Somewhere back in time, we humans flip-flopped the value of the words pride and humility. Pride became the dominant word that we associate with strength, success and deep caring for a cause. Simultaneously, the word "humility" became a descriptive word for really kind, likeable people who put the needs of others ahead of their own. But, if we're honest, we might also think of this attribute as weakness or milquetoast. We would all agree that being a humble person is an aspirational quality, but it certainly doesn't conjure the same images of strength or extraordinary accomplishment as does its cousin pride, especially in business.

This chapter hopes to reset the time continuum and restore humility to its rightful place as quite possibly the greatest strength of all and one that lives at the pinnacle of success and accomplishment. The best place to begin the case is by asking Messieurs Merriam and Webster for definitions:

pride (n) – 1. inordinate self-esteem. 2. a reasonable or justifiable self-respect. 3. delight or elation arising from some act, possession, or relationship.

humility (n) – 1. freedom from pride or arrogance: the quality or state of being humble

humble (adj) – 1. not proud or haughty: not arrogant or assertive

Pride in and of itself is not a bad thing. Like most things, we mess it up with our humanness. We can be and should be proud of our accomplishments, our children, our spouse, our team at the office, our home, etc. That is all perfectly wonderful and healthy. The pride that we are focusing on is the one that quietly destroys us from the inside out. Destructive pride, and we are all guilty of this form of pride, occurs in the seemingly endless, almost obsessive, focus on oneself (our job, neighborhood, friends, clothes, bank account, car . . .) as a measurement of our self-worth. It comes in two forms; a superiority sense of pride and an inferiority sense of pride. Superiority says, "Look at me! I'm better at . . . or have more of . . . etc.," and the feeling fuels our sense of self. Inferiority says the opposite: "Look at him! He is better at . . . or has more of . . . etc.," and it crushes our confidence and nullifies our accomplishments. Both are equally destructive, and (speaking for myself here) we tend to vacillate between the two countless times a day. It's schizophrenic narcissism. This kind of pride makes you want to do great things, be a part of great teams, because you want everyone in the world to look at you and think, "Wow! You're really great!" and you want to agree, "Yes. I am really great." Or, it keeps you from making the effort in the first place for fear of failure and/or your own lack of confidence in your value and abilities.

C. S. Lewis said, "Pride gets no pleasure out of having something, only out of having more of it than the next man . . . It is the comparison that makes you proud: the pleasure of being

Humility

above the rest. Once the element of competition is gone, pride is gone." What he so eloquently articulated, a fact that we all must agree with once our worldview is expanded, is that we walk through life constantly comparing ourselves against some fictitious scoreboard. When we score well against the mean, we are happy. When we score poorly, we're sad and then we lose sight of the value of the accomplishment, or thing, or person. Our destructive pride creates a vicious cycle that leads ultimately to dissatisfaction and a lack of fulfillment. Theodore Roosevelt beautifully said, "Comparison is the thief of joy." He could not have been more right.

Truly humble people, on the other hand, also want to do great things, to be a part of great teams (they are no less ambitious), but they do so because they enjoy the thing itself, are good at it, and/or want to see the joy in the team's accomplishments, to solve a problem for others, to launch those around them, to add value to the greater whole. The difference between pride and humility is not success or failure, strength or weakness. The difference is purely motivation and the narrative that plays out in one's own mind. A humble person is really fine with someone else getting credit. They share joy in others' success rather than growing bitter through jealousy and a desire for the limelight. They relish in helping others grow, pushing people's careers, seeing them reach their full potential even if it's greater than their own. They have friends for the sake of the relationship rather than as a means to increase their social standing. They seek constructive criticism and earnestly desire to improve. If you've ever asked someone for feedback and then gotten angry or defensive when they were honest about your weaknesses, you have a pride problem. I'm quite certain that most of us will agree that we are guilty as charged.

It is terribly ironic that "pride" is the stronger word in our culture, when a truly humble person is a giant of strength, self-confidence, and self-worth who has no need to have their ego stroked. A prideful person lives for it and is crushed when the image they've worked so hard to create is tarnished or loses value. It is equally ironic that truly humble people wield a far greater stick of influence than those maniacally managing their pride. Others trust the humble, for they genuinely care and will run through walls for them because the feeling is mutual. All of which has a beautiful way of bringing the virtuous cycle back to success for the one who embraced the strength of humility.

There has been no greater example in my life of the power of humility than the gentleman who is the chairman and CEO of the company that I have worked for all of these years, Carl Sewell Jr. Carl is a business legend in Texas known for his incredibly successful chain of luxury automobile dealerships. He is known around the world for the book that he authored with Paul Brown in 1990: *Customers for Life*. I have never known anyone like him, and it is likely that I never will again. None have done more to contribute to the truly transformational life that has materialized for me than Carl. And trust me when I tell you that I am not alone. In fact, I'm quite confident that

Humility

there would be a list of hundreds, if not thousands, who would say the same if asked.

The thing that makes him so amazing, and such a special person to get to watch and learn from, is not the remarkable level of success that he has achieved in business. It is not his book that has served as the foundational text to many a company around the world nor is it the ways in which he has enhanced or revolutionized the automotive industry. What makes Carl Sewell such an extraordinary person is the way that he goes through life in spite of all of his success and recognition. When viewed through the lens of humility as a trait of the extraordinary, I can think of no better example than this man.

Everywhere that he goes, certainly within the confines of our industry, he is known as one of the best, most knowledgeable and, undeniably, one of the most experienced. But, despite that fact, he is the first to listen, to ask questions, to seek to learn, and to recognize the accomplishments of others. He never assumes his way is the only right way and realizes that an outsider challenging the system might actually know something that he does not. Typically when in the presence of someone at his level, you basically interview them. Clearly, they have the knowledge, wisdom, experience and credibility that tilt the scale in the conversation. It is perfectly natural, but this is not the case with Carl. He is always more interested in hearing from you than the other way around, and it is a genuine interest. His greatest joy is found in learning, helping, encouraging and supporting others. This does not mean that he is not ambitious. In fact, quite the contrary. He is fueled by a desire to be the best. The difference with Carl versus a prideful man is that this desire is for the greater good of the whole, for all of those who he is entrusted to shepherd, rather than as a means to inflate his ego.

Carl Sewell is a man of incredible personal accomplishments. He could easily and understandably let it all go to his head, but he chooses not to. When you spend time with Carl, even if he is giving you difficult feedback, you feel challenged, appreciated and genuinely cared for. True humility in a leader makes those who follow want to do anything and everything to succeed for them rather than in spite of them. True humility is one of the greatest powers that one can possess.

Chapter 1, Responsibility, helped to reshape our worldview into an understanding of the importance of setting a foundation of responsible, disciplined living. Chapter 2, Focus, helped us to explore our dreams, make plans, make commitments, and move from a temporary mental state to a permanent one. Chapter 3, Curiosity, helped us to recognize that our education shouldn't end after high school or college but is just as important to our health and happiness and the achievement of our dreams as a healthy diet and regular exercise. Chapter 4, Humility, helps us to recognize that our pride can be a destructive attribute that prevents us from listening to, learning from, and growing as a result of constructive feedback and negative experiences.

Humility

Furthermore, the negative sense of our pride can cause us to blindly ignore the areas where we struggle and the way we make others feel and/or cause us to push ourselves into the spotlight rather than pushing the spotlight onto others. This is a deep chapter and can be filled with some tough revelations and even tougher conversations. None of us is ever cured of our pride. Rather, we are all at varying levels of awareness of our affliction. We may make great strides in one category of our life only to be laid low the next day in another.

Do not be discouraged! The only difference between a prideful person and a humble one is that the humble person recognizes the fact that they have a problem with their pride. This awareness is now yours, and over time you will begin to develop the superhuman ability to identify when you are negatively motivated by, or negatively affected by, your ego. It is in these moments of revelation that a humble person will stop, think, reevaluate, and move forward in a new, healthy, positive, joy-giving direction.

Here's to joy!

THOUGHTS ON HOW TO EFFECTIVELY USE THIS CHAPTER

WARM-UP WRITING

- Do you have a Carl Sewell in your life? Is there someone who came to mind while you were reading this chapter? If so, write them a letter and tell them about the positive influence and impact they have had on your life by virtue of their example.

TAKE TIME TO THINK AND WRITE ABOUT YOUR STRENGTHS AND WEAKNESSES AS YOU KNOW THEM.

Identify areas of struggle and recognize where you assume a defensive position when challenged.

DOCUMENT YOUR GROWTH.

Talk through the struggles and surprises. Utilize your strengths and either improve upon your weaknesses or use them as opportunities to let others shine at home and at work. Are you holding on to responsibilities that others can do better solely to feed your insecurities? Are you afraid of someone doing it better?

DOCUMENT THE REVELATORY MOMENTS when you recognize that your words, behaviors, or feelings are rooted in the destructive form of pride and you stop to think, reevaluate, and move forward in a new, healthy, positive, humble, joy-giving direction.

Humility

WHEN YOU'RE READY, SEEK FEEDBACK FROM OTHERS.

Start with friends outside of work and family members. Ask for true honesty and assure them that there will be no retribution. Perform the same exercise in your workplace.

Have private conversations or ask them to answer the following questions anonymously on a simple, blank sheet of paper.

Anonymity (especially in the workplace) has a tendency to net more candid results:

- What do you view as my strengths?
- What do you view as my weaknesses?

What all, no matter how trivial it may seem, can I do/change/improve that would make me a more effective employee/leader/peer/friend/parent/spouse/partner?

Keep the results private. Think deeply about the opening remarks and do not allow the information to fuel you or kill you. Learn from the data and pay special attention to the feedback that you immediately disagree with or makes you feel angry or annoyed.

Analyze why. Oftentimes, this is where meaningful growth happens.

ANALYZE EACH BUCKET OF YOUR LIFE

through the lens of the destructive form of pride. Identify ways in which your behaviors, choices, or motivations are an effort to score well against the fictitious scoreboard. Through the lens of humility, how might you respond/react/act/communicate differently?

- Personal life: spouse, children, family, friends, clubs, charitable organizations, affiliations
- Professional life: career, peers, delegation or lack thereof, need for the spotlight or spotlight on others
- Health/wellness: vanity, image
- Personal finances: money, investments, possessions, neighborhood
- Spiritual life/emotional well-being: relationship with God, a higher power, support group, church, memberships

USE YOUR GUERI NOTEBOOK COMPANION OR YOUR OWN NOTEBOOK TO JOURNAL ON THESE QUESTIONS ABOUT YOUR LIFE—PERSONAL, PROFESSIONAL, AND SPIRITUAL.

PRINCIPLE FIVE
Service

5

Service

5

EXTRAORDINARY PEOPLE FIND THEIR JOY IN THE SERVICE OF OTHERS. THEIR HAPPINESS IS TIED TO OTHERS' WELL-BEING. THEY MEASURE THEMSELVES BY THEIR CONTRIBUTION RATHER THAN THEIR ACCUMULATION. THEY LIFT OTHERS UP AND INSPIRE THEM TO ACHIEVE EVER-GREATER HEIGHTS. THEY ARE THE GOLDEN RULE. THEY ARE THE LIGHT.

Service

Undoubtedly, there is a more uplifting way to begin the fifth and final chapter of this project than by reminding us all of our mortality. However, as we come to the close of this journey, or (for some of us) this version of the journey before we begin again, it seems fitting that we should be perfectly frank with each other. The fact is that we will not be here forever. The older we get, the faster time seems to sweep by and we grow to appreciate just how precious each hour, day, month and year truly is. This truth of the human condition is why George Bernard Shaw so keenly pointed out, "Youth is wasted on the young."

Humans run so hard to accomplish much—to find meaning and purpose, fame, and fortune. But, when the final bell tolls, people will remember what you did for them, how you made them feel, how much you cared, the effort you took, and/or the way that you utilized your resources for the benefit of those around you. People are not remembered for how much they accumulated in life, but, rather, how much they gave of their time, talents and resources. Regardless of our age, the sooner we learn to accept the reality that life has a term limit and we channel that sense of urgency against the clock into the things that truly matter (pouring into, supporting, and assisting those around us to achieve their happiest life and greatest levels of success), the more we, too, succeed.

Repetitio est mater studiorum. Repetition is the mother of learning. And so, one final time . . . Chapter 1, Responsibility, helped to reshape our worldview into an understanding of the importance of setting a foundation of responsible, disciplined living. Chapter 2, Focus, helped us to explore our dreams, make plans, make commitments, and move from a temporary mental state to a permanent one. Chapter 3, Curiosity, helped us to recognize that our education shouldn't end after high school or college but is just as important to our health and happiness and the achievement of our dreams as a healthy diet and regular exercise. Chapter 4, Humility, introduced us to the fact that we all struggle with the destructive form of pride and that comparison for ego's sake is the thief of joy. Chapter 5, Service, is dedicated to leveraging all that we have accomplished in order to make a positive difference in the lives of those around us.

The idea of servant leadership as a movement was inspired in a book *The Servant as Leader* written in 1970 by Robert Greenleaf. There is very little more that I could share, outside of personal anecdotes and stories, to better espouse the enduring principles of leadership through service than the man who quite literally wrote the book on the subject. I highly recommend that you invest time reading the full book.

Service

FROM MY NOTES ON THE
LESSONS OF SERVICE FROM THE
MASTER, ROBERT GREENLEAF,
A SERVANT-LEADER:

1. Believes living in service to others is the best use of life and is itself a virtuous cycle.

Helping others succeed is the best strategy for achieving personal development and fulfillment.

"The servant-leader is servant first. . . . It brings with the natural feeling that one wants to serve, to serve first. Then conscious choice brings one to aspire to lead. That person is sharply different from one who is leader first, perhaps because of the need to assuage an unusual power drive or to acquire material possessions."

2. Has a clear vision of where they are going and invites others to come along, even at risk to themselves.

"The very essence of leadership, going out ahead to show the way, derives from more than usual openness to inspiration. . . . But the leader needs more than inspiration. A leader ventures to say: 'I will go; come with me!' A leader initiates, provides the ideas and the structure, and takes the risk of failure along with the chance of success."

3. Listens first and listens to understand.

"When one is a leader, this disposition causes one to be seen as servant first. This suggests that a non-servant who wants to be a servant might become a natural servant through a long arduous discipline of learning to listen, a discipline sufficiently sustained that the automatic response to any problem is to listen first. I have seen enough remarkable transformations in people who have been trained to listen to have some confidence in this approach. It is because true listening builds strength in other people."

4. Accepts people as they are and empathizes with the challenges of life. It does not mean that they will accept poor performance or a lack of effort.

"The servant always accepts and empathizes, never rejects. The servant as leader always empathizes, always accepts the person but sometimes refuses to accept some of the person's effort or performance as good enough . . . deep down inside the great ones have empathy and an unqualified acceptance of the persons of those who go with their leadership. Acceptance of the person, though, requires a tolerance of imperfection. Anybody could lead perfect people—if there were any. But there aren't any perfect people."

Service

5. Understands that all people are in need of healing (including themselves). Servants seek to help people heal, which also serves to heal the healer.

- -

"This is an interesting word, healing, with its meaning, 'to make whole.' . . . Perhaps, as with the minister and the doctor, the servant-leader might also acknowledge that his own healing is his motivation. There is something subtle communicated to one who is being served and led if, implicit in the compact between servant-leader and led, is the understanding that the search for wholeness is something they share."

6. Understands that human service comes with unlimited liability. True trust and respect come from openness, honesty and vulnerability, all of which are uncomfort-able, unnatural and messy.

- -

"Institutions as we know them are designed to limit liability for those who serve through them. . . . Most of the goods and services we now depend on will probably continue to be furnished by such limited liability institutions. But any human service where the one who is served should be loved in the process requires community, a face-to-face group in which the liability of each for the other and all for one is unlimited, or as close to it as it is possible to get. Trust and respect are highest in this circumstance and an accepted ethic that gives strength to all is reinforced."

7. Knows that in order to serve, you must know your own heart first and the effect you have on others. Do you enrich others' lives, are you neutral, or do you take away?

"If there were a dependable way that would tell us, 'These people enrich by their presence, they are neutral, or they take away,' life would be without challenge. Yet it is terribly important that one know, both about oneself and about others, whether the net effect of one's influence on others enriches, is neutral, or diminishes and depletes."

8. Believes that it all starts within. If you want to bring joy to others, you must first find joy in yourself. And, conversely, others cannot bring joy to you.

"A King once asked Confucius' advice on what to do about the large number of thieves. Confucius answered, 'If you, sir, were not covetous, although you should reward them to do it, they would not steal.' This advice places an enormous burden on those who are favored by the rules, and it establishes how old is the notion that the servant views any problem in the world as in here, inside oneself, not out there.

And if a flaw in the world is to be remedied, to the servant the process of change starts in here, in the servant, not out there.... So it is with joy. Joy is inward, it is generated inside. It is not found outside and brought in. It is for those who accept the world as it is, part good, part bad, and who identify with the good by adding a little island of serenity to it."

Service

One of the greatest physical representations of the servant as leader that I have witnessed was that of my late dear friend, Michael Douglas Horn Sr.

In life Doug accomplished much. He was the third-generation owner-operator of a successful manufacturing business, enjoyed 43 years of marriage to the love of his life, Priscilla, was the loving father to three accomplished children, reveled in being "Grandoug" to his four grandbabies, was an elder in his church, was passionately involved in the World Missions program that took him all over the world to serve, was a life member of the Salesmanship Club where he participated in the weekly reading buddy program for many years, and for me, was an outstanding mentor. There are few people that I have known who were more widely read or interesting to talk to. Doug always made himself available and, as Robert Greenleaf described, was an intense listener. It is my aspirational desire to attempt to live in service to my fellow man as well as Doug Horn did. Trust me, he set a high bar.

All of us experience moments that have profound, long-term implications for how we choose to live moving forward. They are seared in our memory, and we can instantly transport ourselves back to that moment. We can see the sights, hear the sounds, and smell the smells as if we were still there. For me, one of those such events was the memorial service of Doug Horn. I knew Doug was a great man, but I didn't fully appreciate just how great he was until I was sitting in church on that hot summer day in Texas.

I suppose it is sad to think about the fact that humans wait to celebrate the accomplishments of a person's life until they are no longer there to hear it. But I'm pretty sure that Doug would never have wanted that type of attention in life. In fact, I'm confident that he wouldn't have understood what all the hubbub was about. His point of view, and what made him so special, was that the way he lived his life was simply the way that he believed he was supposed to. He was just following the rules.

The church was packed to overflowing. Extra chairs had been brought in and were arranged at the end of each pew. There were rows of people paying their respects standing in the back of the sanctuary. I don't know the actual attendance numbers, but my guess would be more than 1,200. The service was beautiful and emotional for all. There were several speakers and many songs, Doug's favorites, which were sung by the congregation. All in all, not all that different than any other memorial service— that is, until the end.

The senior pastor of our church (we are members of the same church as Doug and his family), Mark Davis, stood to share the final thoughts and to close the service. Mark told the story of the first time that he met Doug and a few humorous and emotional stories from the many mission trips that they had been on together.

Service

He described the loving sacrifice that was made by this man and the ways in which he always chose to put the needs of others ahead of his own. And this is when it happened, a physical representation of the impact of the life of a single man in a way that I had never before witnessed. Life-changing for the living.

Mark, fighting back tears at the loss of his dear friend, said, "I would like to take a bit of a risk and do something that I have never done before while officiating a service like this." He went on, "If Doug ever said to you the words 'I love you,' please raise your hand." In response, at least a quarter of the hands in the massive hall lifted. He went on, "If you ever received a phone call from Doug where he sang an earsplitting but deeply heart-felt version of 'Happy Birthday' to you on your birthday, please raise your hand." At this precise moment, at least half of the congregation held their hands aloft. The energy was palpable as folks turned to witness the simple and incredible display of a man's care. Mark went on, "Now, if you personally attended or one of your children attended a Bible study that was taught by Doug, please raise your hand." To this request three-quarters of the congregation's hands were now raised. The murmurs of the crowd began to grow as the bewildered in attendance shared their disbelief at the spectacle with those around them. Again, Mark asked them to lower their hands, and, as if building to a crescendo, he asked his fourth and final prompt, "If you ever, at a time in your life when you either needed comfort or encouragement or both, received words of assurance, prayer, scripture or all of the above from Doug Horn, please stand."

Shockingly, nearly ALL of the people in attendance rose to their feet! All impacted deeply, meaningfully, by a man who cared with all of his heart and mind about being a light in the lives of those around him. It was truly awe-inspiring. Mark closed the service with the masses on their feet by saying, "There you see it. The measure of a man that lived life well." It is a moment that I will never forget.

When we reach the end of our lives, what will matter most to us in those final days, hours, minutes, seconds will not be what we managed to accumulate in our time on earth. That which we will long for most will be the presence of our loved ones and the knowledge that we contributed positively to the lives of others.

It is perfectly human for the accumulation of stuff (titles, money, possessions, etc.) to become a measurement of our self-worth. Where we humans mess this up, and often discover far too late, is that we've been watching the wrong scoreboard all along. The scoreboard we should be watching and what was so clearly displayed at Doug's celebration of life is the depth and impact that we have on people. It's the people that matter. It's the people that result in significance.

It doesn't mean that you shouldn't be ambitious, successful, or wealthy. These things should be used as tools to serve your fellow man. It is how you choose to use the things you have been fortunate enough to possess (including a healthy mind and body) that has sustaining, eternal value. Doug had this figured out.

Service

Extraordinary people are responsible, focused, curious, humble and live in service to their fellow man. Living in service to our fellow man need not be more complicated than simply being kind. Embody the Golden Rule; do unto others as you would have them do unto you.

Let's commit to each other and let our notebook be a physical reminder as we move through life to set a positive example for those around us in all things but especially in the small ones. Let's smile because we have much to be happy about and thankful for. Let's say "hello" to strangers on the sidewalk. Let's look over our shoulder and hold open the door for the person walking in behind us, even if they're a little bit farther away than seems socially necessary. Let's tip well. Let's slow down to let that person with their blinker on merge into our lane. Let's send a wave of "thanks" to the kind soul who lets us merge into their lane. Let's buy the person's groceries that doesn't quite have enough. Let's take a genuine interest in the people we meet, ask them questions because we're curious and we care, and stop trying to find a moment where we can turn the conversation back to talking about ourselves. Let's give up our seat for someone who needs it more than we do.

Let's take time to live, love, laugh, cry, hug, give, and celebrate life with the people in our world.

SPARKS OF INSPIRATION

THOUGHTS ON HOW TO EFFECTIVELY USE THIS CHAPTER

WARM-UP WRITING

- Think back to a moment in your life when you witnessed something, someone told you something, or you had a significant emotional event that, in hindsight, even if only in a small way, changed your life forever. Write about it.

USE YOUR JOURNALING TIME TO WRITE about things, people, opportunities, gifts, experiences, etc., that you are grateful for in your life.

IDENTIFY AN OPPORTUNITY where you can shift the spotlight from you to those around you. Leverage your noble purpose and your unique gifts to improve the lives of others by giving someone a chance to do something that will stretch them beyond their current role or responsibility. Launch someone.

ONE OF THE SIMPLEST WAYS TO PRACTICE THE BEHAVIORS OF A SERVANT IS TO SAY THE WORDS "THANK YOU" SINCERELY AND OFTEN.

- Make a list of the men and women who have exemplified the life of a servant in your world. Write each of them a heartfelt letter. Tell them just how grateful you are for what they have done for you. Never discount the value and importance of a handwritten note.

- During your journal time, identify at least one person in your immediate sphere of influence who deserves to hear you say the words "thank you." Go and do it.

Service

SHARE YOUR MOST IMPORTANT LESSONS LEARNED.

When you finish a book or an article, think of someone who could benefit and send them a copy.

GIVE AN ANONYMOUS GIFT TO A CHARITY OR A PERSON IN NEED.

It doesn't have to be much. Give what you can responsibly afford.

GIVE OF YOUR TIME.

Volunteer for an organization that is serving a purpose meaningful to you. Do it because you want to and not because others will see or be impressed with the gesture. Go somewhere that no one will know who you are. Don't tell anyone (other than your spouse or significant other). Focus on the act of service solely for the sake of serving mankind. Write about the experience and what you learn.

MAKE A LIST of friends and family members where relationships need to be mended. Even if you don't feel at fault, make the effort to reconnect and heal old wounds. Call them. Send them a letter. Forgive.

TAKE AN INTEREST IN OTHERS wherever you go. Strike up conversations with total strangers. Ask them questions and truly listen. Be a genuinely caring citizen of a world full of broken people. Be the light.

MEDITATE AND JOURNAL ON GREENLEAF'S EIGHT POINTS.

With his eight points from *The Servant as Leader*, the master himself, Robert Greenleaf, has provided us with clear buckets to analyze and provocative questions to ask ourselves regarding each. How am I doing? Where can I improve? What steps do I need to take in order to be a greater servant?

USE YOUR GUERI NOTEBOOK COMPANION OR YOUR OWN NOTEBOOK TO JOURNAL ON THESE QUESTIONS ABOUT YOUR LIFE—PERSONAL, PROFESSIONAL, AND SPIRITUAL.

Every morning I rise in disbelief of the life I have today—my wife, children, friends, career. I feel so incredibly fortunate in large part because that has not always been the case. I owe much to my use of this process. But I am acutely aware that life can turn in an instant, and I personally still need a lot of help. I figure I always will. Everything that you read and do in this book has been created as much for me as for you.

Gueri Notes as a process and *A Guide to Self-Disruption* as a book have been made to live life with you as a trusted partner. This is not a book to be read once and then to live out the remainder of its days collecting dust on a shelf. Rather, this book and the Gueri Notes Process should serve as a visible personal commitment to never giving up and always pushing forward, a commitment to continuous self-improvement, a pledge to strive for fulfillment and purpose in life. Everything about this book has been designed with this in mind. It is a resource that is to be carried, written in and referenced often.

THREE

The Partnership

THE PARTNERSHIP

LET ME BE THE FIRST TO CONGRATULATE YOU ON THIS INCREDIBLE ACCOMPLISHMENT. FOR HUMANS LIKE US, COMMITTING TO AND EXECUTING NEW DISCIPLINES FOR AN EXTENDED PERIOD OF TIME IS NO SMALL FEAT. NEVER MIND THE FACT THAT VOLUNTARILY CHOOSING TO PERFORM THIS TYPE OF RADICAL SELF-DISRUPTION IS RARE. IT TAKES A LOT OF COURAGE TO BE THIS VULNERABLE. THIS IS A MOMENT WHERE BEING PROUD IS PERFECTLY APPROPRIATE.

The obvious question is, Where do you go from here?

You may feel that one time through this process has been more than adequate and you have gained the most out of what it has to offer at this time in life. I want you to know that I am honored to have had the opportunity to share the Gueri Notes Process and the principles that have been so transformational and inspirational in my life. It is my great hope that this exercise has served you well on your mountain, that it was timely in this moment of your journey and resulted in clarity, an epiphany or two, deep introspection, great learning, lofty goals, personal and professional growth, new relationships, improved old ones and newfound or renewed feelings of joy. Carry forward and build your own steps and principles. Remember, extraordinary people have a system, and they are fanatical about its use. You are extraordinary.

Some of us, like me, will begin the entire process again . . . and again . . . and again. And, I say this not for self-serving reasons, should you feel compelled to make Gueri Notes and *A Guide to Self-Disruption* a part of your life into perpetuity, you will find that the exercises and the lessons learned will only deepen in value over time. Speaking as the chief notebook ambassador, I can tell you from experience that the repetition of the exercises never grows old. On the contrary, I find that the reminders and the expectations are comforting and inspiring and add a rhythm to life that drives forward progress. Like mustering the strength to press the bicycle pedals when facing a steep incline, no matter how difficult, the steps in the Gueri Notes Process give momentum to my life. The process challenges me to live in a state of continuous improvement, introspection, learning, giving and living. It doesn't stop unless I stop pedaling. The sparks of inspiration from the book feel new each time because life, its circumstances, challenges, people, and opportunities are fluid. The same provocative questions take on an entirely new meaning each go 'round.

No matter which camp you feel you belong in, take great care of your completed notebooks. What you have accomplished to date and what you will add to over the coming years have incredible value and meaning. Whether you believe it now or not, the wisdom that you have to offer the world is priceless; treat it as such. You will want to return to the days, weeks and years that you have traveled, and the learning will only deepen over time. And future generations will learn even more from your trials, tribulations, joys, and victories. I keep mine in a fireproof, waterproof safe.

Create a network. Over the years of using the Gueri Notes Process and your journey through *A Guide to Self-Disruption* and sharing with others, many of my friends and coworkers have adopted the habit. While I have been faithful for more than a dozen years at sending out my annual list of Most Important Lessons Learned, my good friend Jerad Romo began sending me his lessons learned the minute he recapped a book. Along with his list, he shares book recommendations, TED videos, podcasts or any other learning opportunity he feels that I, as well as other friends, would benefit from. I think this is a best practice and is something that I have since added to my personal process. My heart skips a beat when I receive an email from a friend with their wisdom gained. For me, it is like receiving a birthday present! I'm always excited to see what's inside, what treasures await in a wonderful quote, lesson learned, or book I haven't read. Oftentimes the emails are timely, and whether they realize it or not, their lessons are just what I need at a critical moment to help me through a difficult situation.

Experience *A Guide to Self-Disruption* with a friend, a family member, a coworker, or a whole group of them. Meet regularly to discuss your progress through each principle, your break-throughs, challenges, learning moments, etc. There are few things that are more effective at driving meaningful learning, pulling people together, breaking down barriers, and keeping you on track than executing tasks with other humans.

In closing, I would like to leave you with one final challenge: This list of The Five Principles is a good list, but it's certainly not the only one. Each of us is unique in our beliefs and values. As a result, our life-defining principles will vary. As you press on through the next chapters of life, be mindful of this fact and begin to define your five principles. What are the core values that shape how you live a deep and meaningful life? What is the foundation that you want to share and to leave for future generations? With any luck, maybe I will have the opportunity to learn from your incredible life experiences. I am looking forward to it.

BEST WISHES ALWAYS, MY FRIEND.

Klint

ACKNOWLEDGMENTS

"Saying 'thank you' should never be delegated." CARL SEWELL JR.

Before all others, I must thank God for the gift of this process, my incredible family, friends, mentors, and this remarkable life for which I try hard not to take for granted. All things I owe to Him, and through His grace and mercy, He has chosen to lend them out to me for a time. I'm grateful.

Every single day, when I arrive at the office and open my notebook to begin anew, I think of my children. In many ways, the single most important motivating factor for me to complete this project over the past decade has been my three precious babies. Hollis, Margot, and Ryan are truly amazing gifts from God. If you met them, you would certainly agree. I love you all more than I could possibly put into words. I am so proud to be your dad.

My biggest fan. My most valuable critic. The person who always tells me the truth no matter how difficult. The absolute love of my life who steals my breath every time I see her or hear her voice—my wife, Natalie. No one has taught me more than you. I am in awe of the fact that God gave me a partner as incredible as you, and I'm equally stunned by the life and the family that we have built together. I love you with all of my heart. I am so proud to be your husband.

The entire Sewell family. You have heard me say it many times, but the fact remains that everything of value in my life outside of my faith has come as a result of working for this remarkable company. I finished college thanks to your challenge and encouragement. I met Natalie at work. I hadn't traveled outside of the continental United States, and now I have seen the world. My best friends work for the company. You are the ones that expected more of me than I did of myself. I could never possibly repay you for the opportunities, guidance, education, example, and support that you have provided for me. But I promise that I'll try.

In the toughest of times, I had one person who was there to share in the burden, my older brother, Kyle. Bub, I am forever grateful for you. You are the one who created the handful of good memories from my childhood. Because of the 10 years between us, the burden often fell to you to play "dad." That was an unfair position for you to be in since you were just a kid yourself. Nonetheless you were there with a couch to sleep on and help anytime I was in need. Thank you. I love you.

The rest of my family. Sarah and Keith for being such wonderful surrogate parents. Susan and Rick for adding so much joy to our lives. Rachel, Jackson, Cora, Hal, and Dalton for doing life with us. Brandi, Jackson, and Grace, we love you and miss you. The entire extended Guerry family. The entire extended Shults family. All of you have played pivotal roles in my life over the years, and I am eternally grateful. I love you all very much.

Would you believe that I owe much of my success in adulthood to a Pigg and a Kitty? To my amazing high school guidance counselor, Debbie Pigg, and the equally remarkable therapist I went to see when I was 16, Dr. Kitty Harris: I understand that you were doing your jobs and you probably do not even remember me, but I want you both to know that you had a profound impact on my life. Thank you. I'm grateful.

All of my surrogate family and friends back in Lubbock, Texas. The Sittons were the sweet family down the street. I can never thank you enough for your kindness and generosity. You treated me like one of your own. The Greenstreets, the Sanfords, the Eubanks and the Landrums all were equally generous and sweet to me. It has been years since I've seen you, but know that you're not forgotten nor do I take what you all did for me for granted.

My A-Team of Mentors: Carl Sewell, Dr. Jim Denison, Col. Cole Kingseed, and (posthumously) Doug Horn. You all have set an example for me by virtue of the admirable lives that you have lived. Thank you for your time, patience, attention, encouragement, friendship, and leadership. I'm honored to know you.

This group of remarkable gentlemen: Shawn Achor, Bill Hendricks, Dave Gibson, Steve Mulvany and Chris Ullman. Not only are these men dear friends and mentors in their own right, but are also extraordinarily accomplished authors, speakers and businessmen. Each of you has spent hours with me over cups of coffee or bowls of Frito pie or climbing the Rocky Mountains on horseback. I can never possibly repay you for the time you've invested talking, dreaming, reading, editing, adding, critiquing, and generally guiding me through this project. None of this would have been possible without you, and I have loved every minute.

POSTHUMOUSLY:

My mom and dad. Judging by the letter, you may be surprised to find them in this chapter. Our life was tough growing up, but I want you to know that Phil and Lynda were wonderful, loving, smart and talented people. They were both very sick, and sadly it stole their joy, their family, and ultimately both of their lives prematurely. My parents missed out on the best parts of life because of their addictions and their choices. Ironically, I learned so much from their example. Mainly I learned just how easy it can be to slip into destructive behaviors and how important it is for us to remain vigilant in our effort to keep moving forward positively, especially in the toughest of times. I love you and miss you, Mom and Dad.

The original "rock" in my life before all of the others were my mother's parents, Hollis and Lyda Shults. Lord knows I probably wouldn't have survived adolescence without them. You lived The Five Principles. I love you, Mama and Papa.

MOST IMPORTANT LESSONS LEARNED

THIS IS A COLLECTION OF MOST IMPORTANT LESSONS LEARNED FROM MY OWN READING, CONVERSATIONS, TRAVELS, CLASSROOMS, PODCASTS, TED TALKS, MENTORS, AND MORE. SOME I EARNED THE OLD-FASHIONED WAY FROM THE SCHOOL OF HARD KNOCKS, BUT ALL ARE PULLED DIRECTLY FROM THE THOUSANDS OF PAGES OF MY GUERI NOTEBOOKS. I AGONIZED OVER THE ONES TO SHARE WITH YOU, AND I MADE MY BEST EFFORT TO GROUP THEM INTO CATEGORIES THAT FELT APPROPRIATE. I DIDN'T WORRY ABOUT QUOTING SOME FOLKS MORE THAN ONCE; THE LESSON IS WHAT IS IMPORTANT HERE. I HOPE YOU ENJOY THEM AND, MORE IMPORTANTLY, I HOPE YOU FIND A SPARK OR TWO THAT CAN BE ADDED TO YOUR LIST OF MOST IMPORTANT LESSONS LEARNED.

"The best way to predict the future is to create it." Steve Jobs

Dr. Leonard Berry and Kent D. Seltman

Management Lessons from Mayo Clinic

Lessons from the Mayo Clinic: a.) All technology should solve real problems in the context of an organization's core values and culture. b.) Nothing is more important than thoughtfully planning the personalities that make up a team. c.) If your goal is excellence, no artificial incentive can ever match the power of intrinsic motivation. d.) From the customer's perspective . . . an arrogant waiter is an arrogant restaurant. A careless bank teller is a careless bank. e.) Focus on associate's values first and skills second. Competency is irrelevant if we don't share common values. f.) High performing organizations cannot tolerate associates who lack the talent for the positions they occupy.

Jan Carlzon

CEO, SAS Group (1981–1994), retired

"The hardest part of making good business deals is avoiding the bad ones."

Lloyd Provost

Product and process improvement consultant

"Analyzing financial statements will not give you answers, but it will tell you what questions to ask. The ratios themselves are not as important as understanding why the ratios are calculated."

Jim "Mattress Mack" McIngvale

Owner/operator, Gallery Furniture

"Retail should be entertainment for your customers. It should be an experience and not an errand."

Carl Sewell Jr.

Chairman and CEO, Sewell Automotive Companies, author

"When facing a big decision, drag your feet."

Bob Garfield and Doug Levy

Authors, *Can't Buy Me Like*

You cannot take a single relationship for granted, no matter how casual, because within each one resides the benefits of loyalty, labor, ingenuinty and evangelism—not to mention entrée into their social, professional and family circles. This is why you should never give up on trying to right a "wronged" customer or relationship.

Carl Sewell Jr.

Chairman and CEO, Sewell Automotive Companies, author

"Great brands are about what they do—not what they say in advertising."

Denise Lee Yohn

Author, *What Great Brands Do: The Seven Brand-Building Principles that Separate the Best from the Rest*

a.) Start inside—cultivate corporate culture. b.) Avoid selling products—connect with emotions associated with products. c.) Ignore trends—anticipate culture changes, not risky diversions. d.) Don't chase customers—your brand is not for everyone. e.) Sweat the small stuff—the details are what matter most. f.) Commit and stay committed—forgo opportunities for short-term profit that do not align with your brand. g.) Never have to give back—be a part of community, not just a donor for good public relations. h.) Your brand must evolve with the changing, emotional needs of the times.

Sir Richard Branson

Founder, Virgin Group

"Deliberately move your customers' expectations up a few notches and consistently over-deliver on your promises—you will leave your competitors struggling to catch up."

Joe Stallard

Chief human resources officer, Sewell Automotive Companies

"No amount of smiles and gourmet coffee will make up for our inability to satisfy a customer's most basic reasons for visiting our organization."

Horst Schulze

Co-founder, Ritz-Carlton Hotel Company

All customers want three things: a.) zero defects, b.) timeliness, c.) care about me!

Henry Ford

Founder, Ford Motor Company

"If I had asked people what they wanted, they would have said faster horses."

Robert I. Sutton, PhD, and Huggy Rao

Authors, *Scaling Up Excellence*

"Companies grow well and scale badly when they focus on running up the numbers but not the quality."

Michael Dearing

Founder, Harrison Metal

"If you can just let go to the attachment to an outcome, paradoxically, the outcome is better, because you focus on doing your very best work, right in the moment."

Robert I. Sutton, PhD

Author, *Scaling Up Excellence*

"The goal is to build a business that is as beautiful on the inside as it is impressive on the outside. In the end you have to ask, 'Are we happy living in the world we've built?'"

Thomas Edison

American inventor and businessman (1847–1931)

"Anything that won't sell, I don't wait to invent. Its sale is proof of utility, and utility is success."

Horst Schulze

Co-founder, Ritz-Carlton Hotel Company

Three types of customers: a.) Dissatisfied—terrorists. Take pleasure in telling others not to do business. b.) Satisfied—will leave you for a buck. c.) Loyal—need all of your attention. Greatest asset.

Horst Schulze

Co-founder, Ritz-Carlton Hotel Company

"Eliminate defects. We learn from an early age to hide one's defects. You must explain and change that behavior in our associates. Defects waste time and money and hurt customer experiences."

John Brooks

Business Adventures

"There is no accounting for taste. The only dictator of taste that matters is the consumer. They vote with their wallet."

Danny Meyer

Founder, executive chairman, Union Square Hospitality Group

In order to truly be the best, you must first seek to understand what the best is. Be a student of your industry.

Danny Meyer

Founder, executive chairman, Union Square Hospitality Group

"Strive to treat first-time guests better than your competitors treat their loyal customers."

Danny Meyer

Founder, executive chairman, Union Square Hospitality Group

"There is simply no point for me—or anyone on my team—to work hard every day for the purpose of offering guests an average experience."

Danny Meyer

Founder, executive chairman, Union Square Hospitality Group

"People are less forgiving when a winner stumbles than when an up-and-comer stumbles. But a mark of a champion is to welcome scrutiny, persevere, perform beyond expectations and provide an exceptional product—for which forgiveness is not necessary."

Danny Meyer

Founder, executive chairman, Union Square Hospitality Group

"People will say a lot of great things about your business and a lot of nasty things as well. Just remember; you're never as good as the best things they'll say and never as bad as the negative ones. Just keep centered, know what you stand for, strive for new goals, and always be decent."

Danny Meyer

Founder, executive chairman, Union Square Hospitality Group

"Generosity of spirit and a gracious approach to problem solving are, with few exceptions, the most effective ways I know to earn lasting goodwill from your customers."

Carl Sewell Jr.

Chairman and CEO, Sewell Automotive Companies, author

"Anything that we do that the customer doesn't know about has no value."

Danny Meyer

Founder, executive chairman, Union Square Hospitality Group

"How can we become the company that if it existed, would put us out of business?"

Carl Sewell Jr.

Chairman and CEO, Sewell Automotive Companies, author

"The five-year look-back is the best way to understand trends. Month over month doesn't really tell you anything."

Jack Mitchell

Author, *Hug Your Customers*

"Your best customers are the ones that most want for you to do well . . . so it makes perfect sense that you should learn from them."

Dr. Leonard Berry

Management Lessons from Mayo Clinic

Dr. Berry's playbook for retail businesses: a.) Define what great service means in your industry. b.) Major in minors. Do the little things well. Pay attention to the details. c.) Act small even if you're large—quick response, efficiency, communication. d.) Be high-tech and high-touch. Have the latest technology but remember that it is always the people that make the difference for your customers. e.) Invest in alignment. The values of your associates must match the values of the company. f.) Play brand defense not just brand offense. Protect the family name. Be careful about what you associate your company with. g.) Generate social profit. Charitable company activities contribute to a better quality of life for the associates.

Frank Pacetta

Author, *Don't Fire Them, Fire Them Up*

"It is just smart business to collaborate with other groups. Another set of eyes, even if they're not familiar with your business, may bring valuable perspective."

Dr. Frances Frei

Professor of Technology and Operations Management, Harvard Business School

Compete on well-understood pain points. What causes pain in your industry? Remove the pain for your customers.

Dr. Frances Frei

Professor of Technology and Operations Management, Harvard Business School

"Design customer experience around the abilities of the associates you do have rather than the ones you wish you had. Increase the sophistication of your associates or reduce the complexity of the processes."

Dr. Frances Frei

Professor of Technology and Operations Management, Harvard Business School

"Worst to be best—In order to be best in class at something you must be willing to accept that you must be worst in class somewhere else."

Dr. Frances Frei

Professor of Technology and Operations Management, Harvard Business School

"It all starts here: Who do you want to serve and how do you want to serve them?"

"You are what you create, promote, or allow." JACK AND CAROL WEBER

LEADERSHIP

Frank Pacetta

Author, *Don't Fire Them, Fire Them Up*

"Being a leader is hard work; that's why there are so few. It's easier to hunker down behind a desk and be a second-guesser or an absentee landlord who allows his property to fall into ruins while blaming it on the tenants, the termites, or the taxman—anybody but his own negligence."

Frank Pacetta

Author, *Don't Fire Them, Fire Them Up*

"A leader must always be prepared to deliver bad news, to be firm—You must be a leader first and friend second."

U.S. Army War College

Lessons from the U.S. Army War College: a.) Building bench strength is critical to success. It is unsafe and irresponsible to NOT. b.) The price of the effort must match the size of the prize. c.) Leaders set the agenda and sell the vision. Commander's intent: subordinates and superiors—two levels up and two levels down—must have clear instructions outlining vision.

Dr. John Kotter

Konosuke Matsushita Professor of Leadership, emeritus, Harvard Business School; author; founder, Kotter International

What leaders really do: a.) Managers promote stability while leaders press for change. b.) Leaders set a direction. c.) Leaders align people and communicate vision. d.) Visionaries aren't magicians but broad-based strategic thinkers who are willing to take risks.

Tom Baker

Chairman emeritus, Energy

Creating a culture of leadership: a.) Hire those with leadership potential. b.) Expose them early to opportunities to lead, take risks and learn from experiences. c.) Don't be afraid of lateral moves. d.) Create challenging situations for them to learn—special assignments/task forces. e.) Recognize and reward those who develop leaders.

Drs. Jack and Carol Weber

Professors emeritus, University of Virginia, Darden School of Business

At its core, leadership is about altering people's ideas about what is possible and appropriate. Leaders alter worldviews rather than police compliant behavior.

Drs. Jack and Carol Weber

Professors emeritus, University of Virginia, Darden School of Business

When you talk about the future, does it sound like a "call to glory" or a "take your medicine"?

Drs. Jack and Carol Weber

Professors emeritus, University of Virginia, Darden School of Business

In our silence people make stuff up! Usually negative. Communicate often and effectively.

Drs. Jack and Carol Weber

Professors emeritus, University of Virginia, Darden School of Business

Learn to delegate. When you do things that other people can do, you don't have time to do the things that only you can do.

Carl Sewell Jr.

Chairman and CEO, Sewell Automotive Companies, author

"If the most important people are the people on one team, have the most important people picking them."

Jan Carlzon

CEO, SAS Group (1981–1994), retired

"A leader's communication goes well beyond words. It's his lifestyle, dress and behavior."

Col. Cole Kingseed, PhD (Retired)

Professor emeritus of history and Chief of Military History, U.S. Military Academy at West Point

"Leaders must have a restless intolerance for the status quo."

Col. Cole Kingseed, PhD (Retired)

Professor emeritus of history and Chief of Military History, U.S. Military Academy at West Point

"Hope is not a method or a strategy."

Dr. John Kotter

Konosuke Matsushita Professor of Leadership, emeritus, Harvard Business School; author; founder, Kotter International

Aim for the heart—It's never too late to inspire change by speaking to the hearts and minds of our people. Be sincere, thoughtful, and direct. Tell stories to gain connection. Use humor to reduce stress—as long as it's not mean-spirited.

Patrick Lencioni

President, The Table Group; author

Pick a reasonable number of issues that will have the greatest impact and focus on them.

Patrick Lencioni

President, The Table Group; author

One person can change, damage or destroy your culture.

Frank Bettger

American author (1888–1981)

"Enthusiasm is by far the highest paying quality on earth, probably because it is one of the rarest; yet it is one of the most contagious."

Steve Mulvany

Founder and president, Management Tools, Inc.

"If you find an associate with passion for your business, you can't buy it, so you better protect it."

Unknown

People need verbal affirmation from you. They need to hear, I care about you. I'm proud of you. You're good at this.

Steve Mulvany

Founder and president, Management Tools, Inc.

"Instead of waiting for people to earn your trust, give them your trust and let them un-earn it."

Gen. Dwight Eisenhower

Excellent leaders own the decisions they make and the results. "Good or bad, the decision was mine."

Gen. George Patton

"You'll be surprised by the innovation that can occur at the lowest ranks."

Col. Cole Kingseed, PhD (Retired)

Professor emeritus of history and Chief of Military History, U.S. Military Academy at West Point

Combat carries with it a natural motivation and elevated sense of urgency—death. Equally important in business is creating and recreating an elevated sense of urgency.

Gen. Dwight Eisenhower

"The one quality that can be developed by studious reflection and practice is the leadership of men."

Theodore Roosevelt

"The best executive is one who has sense enough to pick good men to do what he wants done, and self-restraint enough to keep from meddling with them while they do it."

Warren Buffett

Buffett's three qualities of a leader: a.) Work ethic, b.) Intelligence, c.) Character—Without the third, the first two will destroy your organization.

Carl Sewell Jr.

Chairman and CEO, Sewell Automotive Companies, author

"Leadership takes presence—not figuratively, but literally. The best fertilizer in a field is a farmer's footsteps."

Dr. Alec Horniman

**Killgallon Ohio Art Professor Emeritus of Business
Administration; Senior Fellow, Olsson Center for Applied
Ethics, Darden School of Business, University of Virginia**

"People are very uncomfortable with feedback because they're
afraid that it'll be averaged."

Dr. Alec Horniman

**Killgallon Ohio Art Professor Emeritus of Business
Administration; Senior Fellow, Olsson Center for Applied
Ethics, Darden School of Business, University of Virginia**

Three "Is" of leadership: a.) Invite, b.) Include, c.) Inspire.

Dale Carnegie

Carnegie principles for delivering a high-impact presenta-
tion: a.) Know the material so well that you own it. b.) Have
a positive feeling about the subject. c.) Project the value and
significance of the project. d.) Stories tell and shape the culture.
Tell more stories.

Unknown

Second-place finishers are by far least satisfied (almost won
but not the winner). Make rewards for second place that are
different and desirable.

Nick Saban

Head football coach, University of Alabama

If you discipline your life, your people, and your systems in very simple consistent ways—all aiming toward a singular purpose—you will win. One play at a time.

Nick Saban

Head football coach, University of Alabama

"Commit to helping every person be their best AS LONG AS THEY WANT TO DO THE WORK."

Alfred Sloan

President, chairman and CEO, General Motors (1875–1966)

"It is impossible to get the measure of what someone can accomplish, until the responsibility is placed on him."

Patrick Lencioni

President, The Table Group; author

Three signs of a miserable job: a.) No measurement—people need to be able to see that they are doing well. b.) Irrelevance—people need to know that what they do matters. c.) Anonymity—people need to know that someone cares about them.

Patrick Lencioni

President, The Table Group; author

When an organization's leaders are cohesive, they create an environment in which success is almost impossible to prevent.

Carl Sewell Jr.

Chairman and CEO, Sewell Automotive Companies, author

"Profound knowledge is the key to making money. Give yourself a goal to gain profound knowledge in a specific area each year."

Steve Mulvany

Founder and president, Management Tools, Inc.

"The questions you ask are more important than the statements you make."

Carl Sewell Jr.

Chairman and CEO, Sewell Automotive Companies, author

Time on task is the greatest indicator of success in a given function. How much T.O.T. are you giving to the most important items?

Battle of the Bulge Medic

Your attitude and your message as the leader (verbal and non-verbal) matter most in times of struggle. "They've got us surrounded! The poor bastards."— Words of an unknown medic at the Battle of the Bulge

Sir Winston Churchill

"Big words are unnecessary when small words will do."

Nick Saban

Head football coach, University of Alabama

Leadership lessons from Nick Saban: a.) Surround yourself with talent. b.) Create a process for everything. c.) Manage the message. d.) Keep it simple. e.) Make wise investments in the future.

Joe Stallard

Chief human resources officer, Sewell Automotive Companies

"The language of a great organization is inherently positive. Listen intently—what you hear will tell you the true heart and culture of your team."

John Daly

Liddell Centennial Professor of Communication, University Distinguished Teaching Professor, and TCB Professor of Management, University of Texas

Great communicators are redundant. Show, tell, do—always offer two examples of a concept.

John Daly

Liddell Centennial Professor of Communication, University Distinguished Teaching Professor, and TCB Professor of Management, University of Texas

Fight to define the problem—whoever wins the problem determines the solution. Really great bosses come up with the problems and let their people fix them. Stop selling solutions to people. Sell problems.

Horst Schulze

Co-founder, Ritz-Carlton Hotel Company

"If you make a mistake, let people know right away! It is not the crime that kills a company, it's the cover-up."

Horst Schulze

Co-founder, Ritz-Carlton Hotel Company

"Without a common goal you're not a team; you just work together."

Joe Stallard

Chief human resources officer, Sewell Automotive Companies

What is your culture? Write a descriptive summary of what you think it is and then ask your associates to do the same, in their own words. Do they match?

Boris Johnson

Author, *The Churchill Factor: How One Man Made History*

"Hitler showed the evil that could be done with rhetoric. Churchill showed how it could help save humanity. Hitler made you feel that he could do anything. Churchill made you feel that you could do anything. The world was lucky he was there to give the roar."

Huggy Rao

"Before you add a new meeting see if there is a meeting you can kill. Same goes for adding rules."

Robert I. Sutton, PhD

Cut cognitive load—companies need more process and structure as they grow. The more you multitask, the dumber you get at everything.

David Kelly

When people are freaked out, focus on the past and the future, not the present. Your job is to keep yourself and your team moving forward. When people are upset with the present: a.) Remind them of a past that ended well. b.) Paint an optimistic picture of the future.

Clarence Francis

Chairman of the board, General Foods Corporation (1888–1985)

"You can buy a person's time; you can buy their physical presence at a given place; you can even buy a measured number of their skilled muscular motions per hour. But, you cannot buy enthusiasm . . . you cannot buy loyalty. You cannot buy the devotion of hearts, minds, and souls. You must earn these."

Robert I. Sutton, PhD

"People who fear their bosses hide bad news and lie about how things are going."

Dudley Haralson (retired)

Group vice president, Sewell Automotive Companies

"In my 45 years in business, I've never see someone fully prepared for advancement. You get the job and you rise to the occasion."

Horst Schulze

Co-founder, Ritz-Carlton Hotel Company

Leaders: a.) Imply that you have a destination in mind. b.) Commit themselves to selling that vision and achieving it. c.) Initiate what it takes to get there. d.) Focus themselves and the organization. e.) Take care of loyal customers. f.) Find new customers. g.) Get more money from them. h.) Find ways to eliminate waste without taking away from the experience.

Horst Schulze

Co-founder, Ritz-Carlton Hotel Company

Profile of a good leader: a.) Healthy ego, b.) Needs to grow intellectually, c.) Works to find the best fit for his people.

Adam Steltzner

Author, *The Right Kind of Crazy: A True Story of Teamwork, Leadership, and High-Stakes Innovation*

There's a vacuum at the top! Great organizations have an insatiable appetite for talented people. If your work is valuable to an organization, you will naturally get sucked to the top.

Danny Meyer

Founder, executive chairman, Union Square Hospitality Group

Danger! "The man's ego could drive him to need to feel important and therefore to surround himself with people with less skill, knowledge, experience, or intelligence than he. This is a recipe for disaster."

Unknown

Don't be afraid to fail . . . as long as we learn something and get better in the process.

Felix Oberholzer-Gee

Andreas Andresen Professor of Business Administration in the Strategy Unit, Harvard Business School

"You will learn a thing or two about your own business by studying companies well outside your norm."

Dr. Frances Frei

Professor of Technology and Operations Management, Harvard Business School

"I have never seen a great organization that doesn't have high standards or a high performing organization that doesn't have performance anxiety."

Len Schlesinger

Baker Foundation Professor, Practice Based Faculty Chair, MBA Field Global Immersion Program Chair, Harvard Business School

"It is our responsibility to obsess about delivering an extraordinary customer experience today and innovating and shaping their journey tomorrow."

Len Schlesinger

Baker Foundation Professor, Practice Based Faculty Chair, MBA Field Global Immersion Program Chair, Harvard Business School

"Never ignore the bookends. The first impression and the last impression you leave with the customer."

Dr. Frances Frei

Professor of Technology and Operations Management, Harvard Business School

"How you spend your time is what matters most. Be ruthless with your time allocation. Be proactive and protective."

Carl Sewell Jr.

Chairman and CEO, Sewell Automotive Companies, author

"At the end of the day it's up to each one of us to do what is necessary to be great."

Nick Saban

Head football coach, University of Alabama

Don't focus on the end result, but rather focus on the processes and systems that lead to results.

Jim Collins

American researcher, author, speaker, and consultant

Get the right people on the bus . . . the wrong people off the bus . . . the right people in the right seats on the bus.

Peter Schutz

President and CEO, Porsche (1930–2017)

"Hire character and train skills."

Danny Meyer

Founder, executive chairman, Union Square Hospitality Group

"The more powerful people become in an organization, the more emotionally intelligent their management skills must become."

Patrick Lencioni

President, The Table Group; author

"The most unhappy people in a company are the ones that don't fit the culture and are allowed to stay."

Randy Baker (Retired)

Group vice president, Sewell Automotive Companies

"We get more people with potential than experience. Success for people with high potential depends on the quality of their teacher."

Danny Meyer

Founder, executive chairman, Union Square Hospitality Group

"When the team is having fun and is focused there is a very good chance that they will win."

Jack Welch

Chairman and CEO, General Electric (1935–2020)

Leadership lessons from Jack Welch: a.) Clearly define the behaviors that equal success. b.) Reward their soul and their wallet. c.) Operate in an open candid environment.

Jack Welch

Chairman and CEO, General Electric (1935–2020)

"As a leader, it's your job to know your people. That's pretty much your only job!"

Unknown

Sharpen a person's strengths before tackling their weaknesses. Attempting to focus attention on one's challenges without first developing a positive bond will unintentionally sabotage growth—it's demoralizing. And even after great rapport is built, coaching on weaknesses should be done so gently.

John Maxwell

Author, *The Maxwell Daily Reader*

"Consistency takes a depth of character that enables people to follow through no matter how tired, distracted or overwhelmed they are."

Unknown

Start a talk with a handful of relevant, possibly humorous stories—they don't have to be about you or have your direct involvement, but they help to get the audience relaxed and engaged.

John Maxwell

Author, *The Maxwell Daily Reader*

"To discover the proper course concerning a poor performer, a leader needs to ask, 'Should this person be trained, transferred or terminated?' The answer will determine the appropriate course of action."

David Novak

Co-founder and former CEO, YUM! Brands

a.) People won't care about you if you don't care about them. b.) The best way to show people you care is to listen. c.) A great idea can come from anywhere. d.) Recognize great work and great ideas anytime and anywhere you see them. e.) Make recognition a catalyst for results. Make it fun! Make it personal! Recognition is universal. Giving recognition is a privilege of leadership. f.) Say "thank you" every chance you get.

Louie Giglio

American Christian pastor, author

"If you don't like the way things are going, change the way you're leading."

Carl Sewell Jr.

Chairman and CEO, Sewell Automotive Companies, author

"Telling isn't teaching."

Carl Sewell Jr.

Chairman and CEO, Sewell Automotive Companies, author

"What is your journey of learning and how do you inspire a journey of learning in others? You cannot dream of things you cannot conceive."

Dudley Haralson (Retired)

Group vice president, Sewell Automotive Companies

"Surround yourself with smart people and build the best team. It's hard to soar with eagles if you're flying with turkeys!"

Joel Nash

Former regional vice president, BMW of North America

"If you're going to play quarterback, you better be able to take a hit."

Jon Gordon

American author and speaker

"We don't get burned out by what we do; we get burned out when we forget why we do it."

Art Grayson

Founder, Grayson Auto Group

"Sometimes your boss doesn't want a pioneer. Sometimes they want nothing more than a soldier. It's your job to understand how they want you to execute your role and then give it to them."

John Maxwell

Author, *The Maxwell Daily Reader*

"Adversity is a crossroads which makes a person choose one of two paths: character or compromise. Every time leaders choose character, they become stronger, even if that choice brings negative consequences."

Klint Guerry

People get their joy from their families. Don't take that away from them.

Major Dick Winters

Commander, Easy Company, Second Battalion, 506th Parachute Infantry Regiment of the 101st Airborne Division, U.S. Army (1918–2011)

Leadership lessons from Maj. Dick Winters: a.) The greatest challenge of a leader is to be fair. We all strive to be, but perception is almost always otherwise. b.) Delegate responsibility to your subordinates and let them do their jobs. You can't do a good job if you don't have a chance to use your creativity and imagination. c.) Remain humble. Don't worry about who receives the credit. d.) Hang tough! Never, ever give up.

Col. Cole Kingseed, PhD (Retired)

Professor emeritus of history and Chief of Military History, U.S. Military Academy at West Point

Leadership lessons from Col. Cole Kingseed: a.) The greatest competitive advantage is a well-aligned team. b.) Leaders who do not communicate and cannot make decisions are ineffective. c.) You can delegate responsibility, but you cannot delegate accountability. d.) Activity does not equate to progress.

Col. Cole Kingseed, PhD (Retired)

Professor emeritus of history and Chief of Military History, U.S. Military Academy at West Point

The leader's message must: respect the past, provide a realistic view on the present, and display an optimistic outlook on the future.

Hal Moore

Lieutenant General, U.S. Army (1922–2017)

Leadership principles from Hal Moore: a.) A leader can do one of two things: 1) inspire confidence or 2) infect the organization with pessimism and indecision. b.) There is always one more thing that you can do to improve your situation. What am I doing now that I shouldn't? What am I not doing now that I should? c.) The only thing wrong when nothing is happening is that nothing is happening. d.) Trust your instincts.

Harvard Business School

What do most people want to see in their leadership? a.) Character—honesty first, b.) Competency—know the business, c.) Vision—strategy, d.) Inspiration—passion

Dr. Frances Frei

Professor of Technology and Operations Management, Harvard Business School

Culture comes down to these three things: a.) monitoring alignment of associates, b.) very rigorous selection process, and c.) intensive (and ongoing) training process.

Dr. Frances Frei

Professor of Technology and Operations Management, Harvard Business School

"Take advantage of the imprinting moments when someone first starts and are a blank canvas. Ask them, 'What do you see and what can we improve?'"

"Avoid placing the burden of your problems on others." UNKNOWN

Dr. Jim Denison

Chief vision officer, Denison Ministries

"Passion is critical to progress. We do best what we care most about. Our priorities empower our purpose."

Judge Edward Bates

U.S. Attorney General (1793–1869)

"Ambition is a force so great to a man that if left unchecked can quietly steal his happiness and his character."

Unknown

You want to make a difference in the world? a.) Be faithful to your spouse. b.) Be the one at the office who refuses to cheat. c.) Be the neighbor who acts neighborly. d.) Be the employee that does the work and does not complain. e.) Pay your bills. f.) Do your part and enjoy life. g.) Don't speak one message and live another.

C. S. Lewis

British author, Anglican lay pastor (1898–1963)

"Giving should cause discomfort and your standard of living should be lower than those with comparable incomes."

Tom Baker

Chairman emeritus, Energy

"It's your responsibility to manage your own career. Let people know what you want to do or where you want to go. Ask them what you need in order to be ready when the time comes."

Unknown

Forcing yourself into uncomfortable situations is the best way to learn and grow.

Unknown

There is no emotion that imprisons the soul more than the unwillingness to forgive.

Drs. Jack and Carol Weber

Professors emeritus, University of Virginia, Darden School of Business

Are you known by your commitments or your complaints?

Drs. Jack and Carol Weber

Professors emeritus, University of Virginia, Darden School of Business

The most accurate description of our identity is what they say about us behind our back.

Dr. Jim Denison

Chief vision officer, Denison Ministries

How to determine when to say yes or no to a request on your time outside of work or family: a.) Am I the only one who can do it? b.) Will there be enduring significance? c.) Does it match my passions? And always remember that someone else's need does not constitute your call. Always beware of the ego biscuits . . . am I doing this because it makes me feel important?

Unknown

The thing you rely on to "take the edge off" becomes your obsession and your depression.

Chip Wilson

Founder, Lululemon Athletica, Inc.

"A daily hit of athletically induced endorphins gives you the ability to make better decisions."

Dr. Jim Denison

Chief vision officer, Denison Ministries

"However black the night, remember; if you haven't quit, you haven't failed."

Unknown

Avoid placing the burden of your problems on others.

Victor Frankl

Author, *Man's Search for Meaning*

"Everything can be taken away from a man but one thing: The last of the human freedoms—to choose one's attitude in any given set of circumstances, to choose one's own way."

J. D. Rockefeller

"A wise old owl lived in an oak, the more he saw the less he spoke, the less he spoke the more he heard. Why aren't we all like that old bird?"

Jim Rohn

American entrepreneur, author, speaker (1930–2009)

"Develop humor without folly. It's OK to be fun, but not foolish."

Richard Foster

Christian theologian

"Although comprehension defines what we are studying, reflection defines the significance of what we are studying."

Charles Dickens

"Electric communication will never be a substitute for the face of someone who with their soul encourages another person to be brave and true."

John Eagle

CEO, John Eagle Dealerships

"All of our good habits come from the bad times and all of our bad habits come from the good times."

Lance Baker

General manager, Sewell Automotive Companies

"The problem with an ego problem is that your ego won't allow you to see that you have an ego problem."

Dennis Rainey

Author, *Stepping Up: A Call to Courageous Manhood*

"The easiest thing for a man to do in a devastating crisis is to move into denial and do nothing."

Dennis Rainey

Author, *Stepping Up: A Call to Courageous Manhood*

"Another good man standing beside you will help you be courageous when journeying through the valley."

Klint Guerry

Every good man needs a great woman who is willing to pop his ego balloons. As painful as it is, thank her often for popping your balloons!

Dr. Alec Horniman

Killgallon Ohio Art Professor emeritus of Business Administration; Senior Fellow, Olsson Center for Applied Ethics, Darden School of Business, University of Virginia

Stop "Thoughting!"—working ahead in your mind without realizing it . . . attempting to answer someone's thoughts before they have them. It's annoying and disrespectful.

Dr. Alec Horniman

Killgallon Ohio Art Professor emeritus of Business Administration; Senior Fellow, Olsson Center for Applied Ethics, Darden School of Business, University of Virginia

"Any emotion that continues beyond the action is a result of 'self-talk.' Beware of the negative narrative that you tell yourself. It's probably not true."

Dr. Timothy Keller

American theologian, author, speaker

Humility is a person's ability to take constructive criticism. To laugh at oneself. To not be above or below another.

Shawn Achor

American author, speaker

"People believe that they have to be successful in order to be happy, but the opposite is true. Happy = Success. Positive = Productivity/Intelligence/Creativity."

Dr. Skip Ryan

Former pastor, Park Cities Presbyterian Church

"Listening is an expression of love. Do you make people feel like the most important person in the world?"

Unknown

When given a directive, you have three options: a.) Do it. b.) Not do it. c.) Respectfully offer another option.

Smokey John

Founder, Smokey John's Bar-B-Que

"Do your giving while you're living so you're knowing where it's going."

Brené Brown

American professor, lecturer, author

"Vulnerability is the core for shame and fear and struggle for worthiness, but it is also the birthplace for joy, creativity, belonging, love and connectedness."

Brené Brown

American professor, lecturer, author

"You cannot selectively numb negative emotion without also numbing the good stuff—joy, happiness."

Carol Dweck

Author, *Mindset: The New Psychology of Success*

What kind of relationships do you want? Those that bolster your ego or ones that challenge you to grow?

Nick Saban

Head football coach, University of Alabama

"If you cannot overcome adversity, learn from your mistakes, and constantly strive for improvement; then you cannot achieve anything significant in life."

Nick Saban

Head football coach, University of Alabama

"You will suffer through one of two things in life; either the pain of discipline or the pain of disappointment."

Jerad Romo

General sales manager, Sewell Automotive Companies

"The difference between persuasion and manipulation is integrity!"

Martin Luther King Jr.

"If a man is called to be a street sweeper, he should sweep streets even as Michelangelo painted, or Beethoven composed music, or Shakespeare wrote poetry. He should sweep streets so well that all the hosts of heaven and earth will pause to say, here lived a great street sweeper who did his job well."

John Daly

Liddell Centennial Professor of Communication, University Distinguished Teaching Professor, and TCB Professor of Management, University of Texas

Make yourself a note and contact a person six weeks after they have lost someone close to them. This is when they will need support the most.

John Daly

Liddell Centennial Professor of Communication, University Distinguished Teaching Professor, and TCB Professor of Management, University of Texas

Develop multiple competencies that surprise people. Makes you more interesting. Opens your mind to more categories. Makes life more fun.

Alyssa Osterhout

College intern (Alyssa gave me this nugget of greatness during her interview!)

Three lessons from Alyssa Osterhout: a.) A simple smile goes a long way. b.) If you are always honest, people will be very forgiving of your shortcomings. c.) You CAN be in three places at one time . . . if you hustle!

Bill Lamberth

Pastor, Young Families Ministry, Park Cities Presbyterian Church

"Love is spelled T.I.M.E."

Natalie Guerry

Spectacular wife and mother; love of the author's life

"When you are gone, people will not remember the specific events and moments, but rather how you made them feel when they were with you."

Horst Schulze

Co-founder, Ritz-Carlton Hotel Company

"Don't be creepy!"

Horst Schulze

Co-founder, Ritz-Carlton Hotel Company

"Polite is easy. Nice takes work."

Dr. Jim Denison

Chief vision officer, Denison Ministries

"You change culture when you reach your highest point of influence and live there faithfully."

Mark Davis

Senior pastor, Park Cities Presbyterian Church

Care for your words. How you talk to people and about people matters.

Mark Davis

Senior pastor, Park Cities Presbyterian Church

Actually help the less fortunate (physically, mentally and with your resources). Not from a distance but with your whole being.

Mark Davis

Senior pastor, Park Cities Presbyterian Church

"Let the challenges and pain of this world into your life without letting the desires of this world into your heart and mind."

Unknown

You must engineer a strategy for learning and reflection, growth and thought.

Joe Stallard

Chief human resources officer, Sewell Automotive Companies

"If learning is drudgery, you're probably doing it wrong."

Benjamin Franklin

"When you're finished changing, you're finished."

Lee Iacocca

Chairman and CEO, Chrysler Corporation (1924–2019)

"If you want to make good use of your time, you've got to know what's important and give it all you've got."

Louisa May Alcott

American novelist (1832–1888)

"I am not afraid of storms, for I am learning to sail my ship."

President Abraham Lincoln

"Most folks are about as happy as they make up their minds to be."

President Calvin Coolidge

"Nothing in the world can take the place of persistence. Talent will not; nothing is more common than unsuccessful individuals with talent. Genius will not; unrewarded genius is almost a proverb. Education will not; the world is full of uneducated derelicts. Persistence and determination alone are omnipotent."

President Calvin Coolidge

"No person was ever honored for what he received. Honor has been awarded for what he gave."

Sir Winston Churchill

"The pessimist sees difficulty in every opportunity. The optimist sees opportunity in every difficulty."

Lou Brock

Major League Baseball outfielder (1939–2020)

"Show me a guy that is afraid to look bad and I'll show you a guy you can beat every time."

Benjamin Franklin

"The U.S. Constitution doesn't guarantee happiness, only the pursuit of it. You have to catch up with it yourself."

Unknown

Courage is not the absence of fear. Courage is moving forward in spite of your fear.

Horace

Roman lyric poet (65 BC–8 BC)

"Adversity reveals genius and prosperity conceals it."

Roger Staubach

Pro football Hall of Fame quarterback, Dallas Cowboys

"It takes a lot of unspectacular preparation to get spectacular results."

President George W. Bush

"There is but one true power and that is the service of others."

Benjamin Franklin

"Industry and patience are the surest means to plenty."

Benjamin Franklin

Ben Franklin's four rules of life: a.) Live debt free. b.) Be honest always. c.) Work hard and don't get distracted by "get rich schemes." d.) Never speak poorly of others.

Doug Lemov

Writer, "Practice Makes Perfect—And Not Just for Jocks and Musicians," *The Wall Street Journal*, October 26, 2012

"Rote learning and conceptual thinking often feed synergistically on each other, freeing our brain capacity for those tasks that require the maximum amount of attention and creativity."

Aristotle

"We are what we repeatedly do. Excellence, then, is not an act, but a habit."

George R. R. Martin

American novelist

"A reader lives a thousand lives. A non-reader only lives one."

Klint Guerry

Never forget the value of a handwritten letter.

James Dobson

Founder, Focus on the Family

"He who dies with the most toys dies anyway."

Valerius Maximus

First-century Latin writer and author

"Frail and fragile surely and like children's toys are the so-called power and wealth of humankind."

Dr. Frances Frei

Professor of Technology and Operations Management, Harvard Business School

"You can either prepare the path for the boy or the boy for the path."

Edwin "Boots" Nowlin Jr.

Senior vice president, Wealth Management, Nowlin, Ferguson, O'Connell, Durham Group

"You get into trouble when you start thinking of yourself as special."

Klint Guerry

Be curious—innovation occurs most frequently when you remain in a constant state of learning. Read. Listen. Ask questions.

Carl Sewell Jr.

Chairman and CEO, Sewell Automotive Companies, author

"A measure of your own integrity is how much time you take to study, learn and make yourself better."

Nelson Mandela

Learn to forgive. "Bitterness is like drinking poison and waiting for your enemies to die."

Stanley Marcus

President and chairman of the board, Neiman Marcus (1905–2002)

"The road to success is paved with mistakes well handled."

Carl Sewell Jr.

Chairman and CEO, Sewell Automotive Companies, author

"Absence does not make the heart grow fonder . . . it makes the heart go wander."

Danny Meyer

Founder, executive chairman, Union Square Hospitality Group

"It's human nature for people to take precisely as much interest in you as you are taking in them."

Matt Chandler

Executive director of the board of the Acts 29 Network, pastor, author

"How many people in your life can give nothing to you? Are you using relationships to try to advance your status or self worth?"

Daniel Kahneman

Author, *Thinking Fast and Slow*

"In order to be the light, one must be in the darkness without conforming to the darkness."

Shankar Vendantam

American journalist, writer, and science correspondent

"We often underestimate our ability to reinvent ourselves."

Unknown

"Enthusiasm, a smile and a sincere desire to put yourself out for a customer do more to build a successful career then all the experience you can ever acquire."

Unknown

"Never lose your temper, and if you do at least hold your tongue."

Benjamin Franklin

"Three may keep a secret if two are dead."

Unknown

"If you are laughed at, try to rise above it. Everyone likes a man that can have a laugh at his own expense. This shows good humor and good sense. If you can laugh at yourself, others will not laugh at you."

William James

American philosopher, historian, psychologist (1842–1910)

"Nothing is so fatiguing as the eternal hanging on of an uncompleted task."

Waite Phillips

American petroleum businessman (1883–1964)

"The trouble with many of us is that we would rather be ruined by flattery and praise than saved by honest criticism."

John Maxwell

Author, *The Maxwell Daily Reader*

"Integrity commits itself to character over personal gain, to people over things, to service over power, to principle over convenience, to the long view over the immediate."

Joe Stallard

Chief human resources officer, Sewell Automotive Companies

"Focus on the job that pays you the best."

Carl Sewell Jr.

Chairman and CEO, Sewell Automotive Companies, author

"Think about your life over the next 20–30 years. The best way to achieve sustained success is to surround yourself with and learn from extraordinary people."

Bobby Moorehead

Manager, Sewell Automotive Companies

"You must take care of yourself in order to take care of others. Like the oxygen mask on an airplane you must put yours on first. You can't save other lives if you are unconscious."

Jason Mayden

CEO, Trillicon Valley

"Do something that is so big that you cannot complete it in your lifetime."

Trog Trogdon

Vice president, Bonton Farms

"Don't stay safe in your little bubble. Change is messy because people are broken. Don't be afraid to get dirty."

Christoph Niemann

Author, illustrator, graphic designer, children's book author

"I'm not done because being done is kind of the opposite of what I'm trying to achieve."

Christoph Niemann

Author, illustrator, graphic designer, children's book author

"Throw in something you think you'll regret and that is usually the most interesting part."

Danny Meyer

Founder, executive chairman, Union Square Hospitality Group

"Each of us tend to overestimate what can be accomplished in one year. And we tend to underestimate what can be accomplished in 10 years."

Les Wexner

Chairman emeritus, Bath & Body Works, Inc.

"When you stop to smell the roses is when you get hit by a truck."

Bryan Baker

Sales associate, Sewell Automotive Companies

"The world is round so people come back around. Be thoughtful about how you leave all conversations and relationships."

John Maxwell

Author, *The Maxwell Daily Reader*

"You can feel a lot about which direction your life is heading by looking at the people with whom you've chosen to spend your time and share your ideas."

Dennis Hamilton

Manager, Sewell Automotive Companies

"Your career isn't going to wipe your chin when you get old."

Doug Maclay Sr.

The father of a friend of the author (1927–2011)

"When the wind ceases to blow . . . ROW!"

Jason McCann

Co-founder, CEO, Vari

"You learn a lot about people when you make money with them. You learn even more when you go broke together."

Unknown

"Be thankful for problems. If they were less difficult, someone with less ability might have your job."

Walter Isaacson

Author, *Leonardo da Vinci*

"Leonardo's genius was a human one, wrought by his own will and ambition. It did not come from being the divine recipient, like Newton or Einstein, of a mind with so much processing power that we mere mortals cannot fathom it. Leonardo had almost no schooling and could barely read Latin or do long division. His genius was of the type we can understand, even take lessons from. It was based on skills we can aspire to improve in ourselves, such as curiosity and intense observation. He had an imagination so excitable that it flirted with the edges of fantasy, which is also something we can try to pursue in ourselves and indulge in our children."

Walter Isaacson

Author, *Leonardo da Vinci*

"Paper turns out to be a superb information storage technology, still readable after 500 years, which our own tweets won't likely be."

Walter Isaacson

Author, *Leonardo da Vinci*

"Above all, Leonardo's relentless curiosity and experimentation should remind us of the importance of instilling, in both ourselves and our children, not just received knowledge, but a willingness to question it—to be imaginative and like talented misfits and rebels in any era, to think different."

Stephen Duneier

Founder and CEO, Bija Advisors LLC; lecturer at University of California; artist; author

"Humans have a natural predilection for achieving and mastering a state of cognitive ease and for avoiding cognitive strain wherever possible. You cannot avoid cognitive strain. You can, however, invite cognitive strain on your own terms. The key is to plan behaviors not the outcome."

Itzhak Perlman

Israeli-American violinist

"The problem with a grand investment or a lifelong obsession is that you don't know whether it was a fortune or folly until the very end."

Carl Sewell Jr.

Chairman and CEO, Sewell Automotive Companies, author

Speaking lessons from Carl Sewell Jr.: a.) Watch your pace. If you speak too fast, it either means you're nervous or insincere. b.) Master the pause. When you have a great point or something important to say, pause and let your audience engage before delivering the message. c.) Speak to your audience like they're your teammates.

Frank Pacetta

Author, *Don't Fire Them, Fire Them Up*

Don't be late for meetings. Punctuality is a common courtesy.

Frank Pacetta

Author, *Don't Fire Them, Fire Them Up*

Dress and groom yourself so you look like a superior product.

Frank Pacetta

Author, *Don't Fire Them, Fire Them Up*

If you don't like your job, find a new one.

Steve Mulvany

Founder and president, Management Tools, Inc.

"A real friend stabs you in the front."

Unknown

Every person that you encounter—the beggar on the street corner, the guy at work with no depth and always a dirty joke, your biggest adversary—they were all molded by God. They can change. Love them. Show them who Jesus is through your words and your actions.

Unknown

Jesus is clear that you must pick a side. You can't be a sheep and act like you're a wolf when you're with wolves.

Saint Augustine

Roman theologian and philosopher (354–430)

"You have made us for yourself and our heart is restless until it rests in you."

Unknown

He loves you no matter what, but God is a strict disciplinarian. Listen and learn.

Holy Bible

Much is expected of those to whom much is given!

Nancy Spiegelberg

American author

"Lord, I crawled across the desert with an empty cup . . . if only I'd known you better I would have come running with a bucket."

"In our fear we bury our talents in the sand." MARK DAVIS

C. S. Lewis

British author, Anglican lay pastor (1898–1963)

"Every child will someday wonder, 'What is the purpose of my life?' Some search for meaning in a career. They opt to be a human 'doing' instead of a human 'being.' Who they are is about what they do; consequently they do a lot. They work many hours because if they don't work they don't have an identity. For others, who they are is what they have. All are mirages in the desert of purpose. Everything you need and want is found in God. We are significant not because of what we do but because of who we are."

Unknown

All people are made in the image of God. Look deeply into their eyes and you will see Him—even if they don't believe.

President Abraham Lincoln

"I have been driven many times to my knees by the overwhelming conviction that I had nowhere else to go. My own wisdom and that of all about me seemed insufficient for the day."

Smokey John

Founder, Smokey John's Bar-B-Que

"You have been set free from something and you are the best person on earth to speak the word to others suffering from the same afflictions."

Unknown

Nothing can ever fill the God-shaped hold in your soul except for God himself. Humans try in vain to fill it with power, money, sex, status—anything but God—only He will ever/ can ever satisfy.

Matt Chandler

Executive director of the board of the Acts 29 Network, pastor, author

"The man who tries to white knuckle his way through behavior modification is fighting a losing battle. Only God can heal!"

Nick Saban

Head football coach, University of Alabama

"How do you pray? To be blessed or to be a blessing?"

Klint Guerry

God did not die so that we could live in comfort. He did not die so that we could be comfortable and entertained. To give into all pleasures. He died so that we may live to pick up His cross and follow Him!

Unknown

God loves "Nobodys!"

Dr. Gary Cook

Chancellor, Dallas Baptist University

"Never forget to be grateful for what the Lord does for you and make every effort to pay it back. You'll never be able to redeem the debt you owe, but you should sure try."

John Owen

English Nonconformist church leader, theologian (1616–1683)

"You need to be killing sin or sin will be killing you."

Dr. Julian Russell

Teaching elder, PCA

What your flock needs from you most: a.) Be an example. Be covered in His Holiness. b.) Examine your motives as a shepherd, not for selfish gain. c.) Point people every day to the Chief Shepherd. You are not it! d.) The sheep bite. Do not be discouraged. Be faithful to the Chief Shepherd.

God

"You need to get your mind off of your wounded pride and get your mind on what is right in my eyes."

Dr. Pete Deison

President, Park Cities Presbyterian Church

"You are not the source of light. You are a reflection of the light."

Mother Theresa

"God hasn't called us to be successful. He called us to be faithful."

Unknown

God calls us to things for His glory and our joy.

Mark Davis

Senior pastor, Park Cities Presbyterian Church

"The real trouble begins when our sin ceases to trouble us."

Mark Davis

Senior pastor, Park Cities Presbyterian Church

"In crisis we have the opportunity to turn toward God or to turn toward man. It's a trait of fallen man to trust only what we can see."

Dr. Timothy Keller

American theologian, author, speaker

"Everything you worship, other than God, will eat you alive."

Dr. Jim Denison

"Is God the King of your life or a hobby?"

C. S. Lewis

British author, Anglican lay pastor (1898–1963)

"Those who put themselves in His hands will become perfect. The change will not be complete in this lifetime. The process is painful."

Unknown

When the Lord tests us, He always tests our limits.

Unknown

The more you grow, the more you realize just how much you do not know and how weak you really are. And, therefore, the more you realize just how much you need God.

Dr. Darrell Bock

Executive Director of Cultural Engagement, The Hendricks Center, Dallas Theological Seminary

"Our armor for battle is our character and our theology."

John Maxwell

Author, *The Maxwell Daily Reader*

Leader's checklist—from the fruit of the spirit: a.) Love—Is my leadership motivated by love? b.) Joy—Do I exhibit an unshakeable joy regardless of life's circumstances? c.) Peace—Do people see my peace and take courage? d.) Patience—Do I wait patiently for results as I develop people or goals? e.) Kindness—Am I caring and understanding toward everyone I meet? f.) Goodness—Do I want the best for others and the organization? g.) Faithfulness—Have I kept my commitments? h.) Gentleness—Is my strength under control? Can I be tough and tender? i.) Self-Control—Am I disciplined to make progress toward my goals?

Steve Green

President, Hobby Lobby Stores, Inc.

"Only one life soon to pass. Only that done in Christ will last."

Steve Green

President, Hobby Lobby Stores, Inc.

"You can't outgive God . . . but you should try!"

William Wilberforce

British politician (1759–1833)

William Wilberforce's seven principles of life: a.) Let your whole life be animated by a deeply held, personal faith in Jesus Christ. b.) Listen for your calling and let your conviction drive both your secular and spiritual life. c.) You cannot change the world alone! Band with like-minded friends and work together in chosen ventures. d.) Ideas and moral beliefs change culture. e.) Being convicted to a cause comes at a steep cost. f.) Let your labors and your faith be focused on the people they affect. g.) Look for strategic partnerships irrespective of differences over methods, ideology or religious beliefs to further the common good.

John Maxwell

Author, *The Maxwell Daily Reader*

Evaluate your leadership as Christ led the Church: a.) Initiative —Do I give direction and take responsibility? b.) Intimacy— Do I experience intimacy with God and others through open conversations? c.) Influence—Do I exercise biblical influence by encouraging and developing others? d.) Integrity—Do I lead an honest life unashamed of who I am when no one is looking? e.) Inner circle—Do I exhibit the fruit of the spirit in my life, including self-discipline?

Mark Davis

Senior pastor, Park Cities Presbyterian Church

"His sheep. His flock. Watch His sheep. Feed His flock. Let the flock see Christ in you as a shepherd."

Unknown

There is nothing you are hiding in that Jesus cannot deliver you from. We all need saving!

"Once you have started on the road of your calling, you cannot stop the train even if you wanted to. It is God's choice." C. S. LEWIS

50 GREAT BOOKS

BOOKS. BOOKS. SO MANY BOOKS.

AN ENDLESS SUPPLY OF KNOWLEDGE

IF TIME IS MADE TO LOOK.

PICKING FAVORITES, AN IMPOSSIBLE TASK.

EACH HAS VALUE AND VIRTUE

SHOULD YOU JUST ASK.

THIS LIST OF 50, A GREAT PLACE TO START.

MAKE READING A PASSION.

IT'S A HABIT THAT'S SMART.

A Sense of Urgency
John P. Kotter

Blink Malcolm Gladwell

Customers for Life Sewell
and Paul B. Brown

Good to Great Jim Collins

**How the Mighty Fall: And
Why Some Companies
Never Give In** Jim Collins

Hug Your Customers
Jack Mitchell

**Management Lessons
from Mayo Clinic**
Leonard L. Berry and
Kent D. Seltman

Outliers Malcolm Gladwell

Setting the Table
Danny Meyer

The Advantage
Patrick Lencioni

The Founder's Mentality
Chris Zook and James Allen

**The Knowing-Doing
Gap** Jeffrey Pfeffer and
Robert I. Sutton

Uncommon Service
Frances Frei and
Anne Morriss

**Empire of the Summer
Moon** S.C. Gwynne

Washington: A Life
Ron Chernow

John Adams David
McCullough

Lincoln the Unknown
Dale Carnegie

Mayflower Nathaniel
Philbrick

The Prize Daniel Yergin

Too Big to Fail
Andrew Ross Sorkin

The Boys in the Boat
Daniel James Brown

Unbroken Laura
Hillenbrand

Undaunted Courage
Stephen Ambrose

**Beyond Band of
Brothers** Dick Winters
and Cole C. Kingseed

D-Day Stephen Ambrose

**The Killer Angels,
Gods and Generals,
The Last Full Measure
(Three Books)** Michael
Shaara and Jeff Shaara

Team of Rivals Doris
Kearns Goodwin

**Lion; Winston Spencer
Churchill: Defender**
William Manchester
and Paul Reid

Man's Search for Meaning
Viktor E. Frankl

**The Millionaire Next
Door** Thomas J. Stanley,
PhD, and William
D. Danko, PhD

**Chop Wood Carry Water:
How to Fall in Love with
the Process of Becoming
Great** Joshua Medcalf

Find Your Whistle
Christopher Ullman

Happiness Advantage
Shawn Achor

The Art of Possibility
Rosamund Stone Zander
and Benjamin Zander

Big Potential Shawn Achor

David and Goliath
Malcolm Gladwell

Good Boss, Bad Boss
Robert I. Sutton, PhD

**Leadership and
Self-Deception** The
Arbinger Institute

Mindset Carol Dweck, PhD

**Now, Discover Your
Strengths** Marcus
Buckingham and Donald
O. Clifton, PhD

Radical Candor Kim Scott

Start with Why
Simon Sinek

The Energy Bus
Jon Gordon

**The Four Obsessions
of an Extraordinary
Executive** Patrick Lencioni

**The Three Signs
of a Miserable Job**
Patrick Lencioni

The Triangle of Truth
Lisa Earle McLeod

Bringing Up Boys
Dr. James Dobson

Every Good Endeavor
Timothy Keller

**The Freedom of
Self-Forgetfulness**
Timothy Keller

The Meaning of Marriage
Timothy Keller

YOU CAN REACH ME AT
KLINT@GUERITOOLS.COM